D0201566

"Why do you call me 'Lord, Lord,' and not do what I tell you?"
"Take heed then how you hear."

LUKE 6:46, 8:18

Related Studies by R. E. O. White

The Stranger of Galilee

The Night He Was Betrayed

Beneath the Cross of Jesus

Five Minutes with the Master

The Mind of Matthew

Luke's Case for Christianity

Enjoying the Gospel of John

Listening Carefully to Jesus

R. E. O. WHITE

WILLIAM B. EERDMANS PUBLISHING COMPANY
GRAND RAPIDS, MICHIGAN / CAMBRIDGE, U.K.

© 2000 Wm. B. Eerdmans Publishing Co.

255 Jefferson Ave. S.E., Grand Rapids, Michigan 49503 /

P.O. Box 163, Cambridge CB3 9PU U.K.

All rights reserved

Printed in the United States of America

05 04 03 02 01 00   7 6 5 4 3 2 1

ISBN 0-8028-4397-2

Contents

A Primer for Disciples

I HAVE INTENDED this brief study of the teaching of Jesus especially for those new to the Christian life, though older Christians too may appreciate fresh insights into Jesus' meaning. I begin with a few aids to understanding Jesus' style of speech and methods of instruction and follow with some account of what he had to say on issues of contemporary importance.

The Revised Standard Version (RSV) of the Gospels is my main reference, though the New International Version (NIV) and the New English Bible (NEB) are consulted. To avoid tedium and unnecessary interruption, Scripture references are given only where quotations may be unfamiliar; a Bible concordance will help in finding others.

I

Jesus the Teacher

I T WAS AS A TEACHER, "lay" and untrained, that Jesus first appeared in public. Of course he was and is more than that. But there is little meaning in calling him Master and Lord if we do not know what he was like, or what he wants us to think, to be, and to do. His teaching and example set the ruling pattern of all Christian living, and both are before us still in the four Gospel records. Yet popular conceptions of Jesus can be hopelessly inadequate, sometimes completely wrong. That is why it is necessary to "take heed how we read."

Jesus taught, when invited, in various synagogues, on open hillsides, beside the sea, occasionally as a guest in large houses, in the public courts of the Jerusalem temple, and in private conversations. Everywhere hearers "wondered at the gracious words which proceeded out of his mouth" (as Luke says); the crowds "were astonished at his teaching, for he taught them as one who had authority, and not as their scribes." Even public officials, well used to hearing speeches by the nation's leaders in the Jewish Sanhedrin, confessed of Jesus that "never man spake like this man."

So we read that "the great throng heard him gladly," finding no difficulty in attending or understanding. But Jesus, of course, spoke their language, was of their time, one of them. We read his words in another language, another age, a very different world, with totally different presuppositions and centuries of debate behind us clouding his meaning. However gladly *we* listen, it needs a little more attention and informed understanding, now, to catch his precise intention.

That is why it is necessary sometimes to pay attention not only to what Jesus says but to how he says it. To speak of his teaching "style" would suggest a formal, studied preparation of speeches; that would be wholly misleading. Jesus himself advised against such overpreparation: "out of the overflowing of the heart the mouth speaks." Other teachers of Jesus' day made much of subtle interpretation of texts, legal niceties, fastidious literalness of interpretation, often bewildering to the common people. In contrast, his teaching was marked by a free, earnest spontaneity that gave authority and grace — and sometimes sharpness — to his words.

Even the simple word "teacher" may be misleading when applied to Jesus. We must put out of mind all thought of classroom, lecture hall, or pulpit. In the synagogue service, after the exposition of the Law, any pious layman, visiting scribe, or Pharisee might be invited to speak or initiate discussion. The same informality — responding to inquiries, current events, criticisms, or opportunities — occasioned much that Jesus said.

One of the most skilled students of the Gospels urges that to approach the teaching of Jesus properly we should first appreciate the utter friendliness of the teacher. He chose his men for their company — "to be with him." At a moment of strain he urged them to "come apart" privately and rest awhile. To one of them he said, "Satan has desired to sift you like wheat, but I have prayed for you." Jesus allows these friends to repeat to him criticism they have heard or to ask him for further explanation of sayings and parables they should have understood. He lets them manage the boat while he sleeps, to go ahead into villages to arrange hospitality, to prepare the final Passover meal. In the garden of Gethsemane he deliberately opened the way for them to escape: "If you seek me, let these men go."

"He is at the service of the lowest," accepts their help, tells them

gratefully, "You are they who have continued with me in my temptations. . . . I have greatly desired to eat this Passover with you before I
suffer." Jesus' own word for those closest to him whom he teaches is
not "students," "audience," or even "disciples," but the essentially
comradely, warmhearted "boys" or "lads." (The original word does
mean "little ones," but was used also by a respected person "to those in
familiar relationship with him.") At the last, Jesus prayed most earnestly for these men and their future. As John says, "Jesus, having
loved his own . . . loved them unto the end." And into their hands he
finally entrusted his own mission.

Such is the context in which Jesus' less public teaching is set: a
friendly, loving relationship, living together in growing understanding, kindling minds. Yet this must not be understood sentimentally.
Even to the disciple with whom Jesus had (apparently) the warmest
sympathy, he could still say when necessary, "Get behind me, you are a
hindrance. . . ." The kindest of teachers, he was still Master and Lord,
while his companions had a great deal to learn — and to unlearn.

And to those beyond this inner circle Jesus was likewise open,
free, approachable, never reserved or constrained. He responded immediately to almost every request, listened when questioned or challenged, appreciated the great faith of a Roman centurion, the wit of a
Syrophoenician woman, the frankness of a puzzled young man ("Jesus
looking upon him loved him"), attracted children to himself and defended their exuberant singing, at once felt and reassured the despair
of Jairus at the news his daughter had died, and spoke gently to a shy
woman who touched his cloak from behind. He was in no sense a "private" person.

And in such moments Jesus always gave of himself freely, without concealment. He showed his disappointment when some turned
away; his weariness, sighing deeply at others' obtuseness; his deep indignation when his Sabbath healings were rebuked for trivial reasons;
his anger when callousness or contempt was shown to the needy or the
sinful. He did not out of pride hide compassion or pity toward lepers,
the insane, the bereaved, nor his own suffering ("I have a baptism to

undergo, and how distressed I am until it is completed," NIV). Being "in an agony, he prayed more earnestly." And he shared also his moments of exultation, "rejoicing in spirit" — "I thank Thee, Father. . . ."

Such then was the Teacher: what of the sources available for his teaching?

2

The Sources

L UKE TELLS US clearly that by his time (probably the 80s of the first century) many had "undertaken to compile a narrative" of the life of Jesus as "delivered to us by those who from the beginning were eye-witnesses and ministers of the word." It seemed good to him also, "having followed all things closely for some time past, to write an orderly account . . ." (1:1-4). It is these personal memories of Jesus, told and retold in local Christian assemblies by individuals recalling what Jesus did or said in their towns, villages, synagogues, or homes, that Luke had researched, collected, and arranged into his "orderly account."

In all probability, our Gospels began to appear in the 60s AD (Mark) through the 80s (Matthew and Luke), with John at about 90 AD. Thus, for about a generation or longer, the first Christians relied upon this many-times-retold oral tradition about Jesus, helped by the Holy Spirit who, Jesus promised, would "bring all things to their remembrance." Many scholars think that both Matthew and Luke were helped by an early written collection of some of Jesus' sayings, which both reproduce in similar words. We know, too, that Paul had learned things Jesus said, about laborers for the gospel deserving wages; about the blessedness of giving; about marriage (carefully distinguishing the

Lord's words from his own advice); and concerning the original Lord's Supper, which came to him "of the Lord" evidently through those who were there.

It is interesting, and sometimes illuminating, to consider the way in which the separate memories of Jesus would be appealed to in discussions of actual problems facing the first Christians. How should Gentile Christians — or Christian Jews — treat the Jewish Sabbath laws? What did Jesus do, and say? The answer to such questions lay in certain "pronouncement stories" ending in definitive statements by the Lord: on Sabbath, Mark 2:23-28; on "unclean" foods, Mark 7:14-19; on adultery, Mark 10:1-9; on paying taxes to Caesar, Mark 12:13-17, are clear examples.

Miracle stories would be treasured and retold by those healed or by their descendants and witnesses, to encourage new patients. Stories centering on Jesus himself — his baptism, temptation, rejection at Nazareth, transfiguration, and the like — were always welcomed and had spiritual value for new converts. And the story of Jesus' death would be repeated (as Jesus intended) continually in the Lord's Supper. We can see, too, that groups of sayings linked by key words would be recalled (Mark 9:49-50 is such a group — things Jesus said about salt). Parables would be remembered often, probably prompting interminable discussion! So each remembered incident or saying would speak to contemporary situations in the early church — and tended to be repeated more often when it did so.

It is not surprising that information passed from person to person for so long should vary in detail when finally written down, despite the remarkable power of memory in nonreading societies. A further cause of variation is the need of translation: sayings recalled at first in Jesus' own language (probably Aramaic, the common speech of Palestine) would be translated into Greek for the later churches of the Gentile world. These were preserved in Greek in our Gospels, and come down to us in the English of the sixteenth and seventeenth centuries (the King James, or Authorized, Version [AV]) and in numerous versions since. In this study we use primarily the modern Revised

Standard Version (RSV), with occasional help from the New International Version (NIV) and the New English Bible (NEB). This variety in translation cautions us to compare the four Gospels one with another and never to press too firmly on one or two English words in some favorite version just because "we like that translation." It is astonishing how rarely we are left in doubt of Jesus' meaning.

One further feature of our sources for Jesus' teaching must be mentioned. The Gospel writers wrote for their own readers, not for us. Each used the information that came to him for a different audience and situation. Mark, about 65 AD, addressed a mixed Jewish-Gentile church at Rome, probably recording what Peter taught there, mainly events rather than Christ's teaching. Matthew addressed a mainly Jewish church, probably at Antioch, obviously concerned that his church should know thoroughly the teaching of Jesus, arranging his sayings into five great "discourses" (chaps. 5–7, 10, 13, 23, and 24–25), with many warnings about "little faith," disobedience, and false profession. Luke wrote for Gentiles like Theophilus, recommending to them the new Christian movement. John wrote probably for Ephesus and its environs, about 90 AD — long after the church's links with Jewry were severed — producing a very different version of the same story after long reflection on its deepest implications.

It is fascinating to notice, for example, that Luke sometimes gives a saying of Jesus in a more illuminating setting than does Matthew: compare Luke 11:1-4 with Matt. 6:9ff. (the Lord's Prayer); Luke 15:3-7, Jesus answering criticism of his friendship with sinners, with Matt. 18:10-14, the church needing to care for erring Christians (the seeking shepherd); Luke 16:13, a comment on the parable of the embezzling steward, with Matt. 6:24 in the "sermon on the mount" (impossible to serve God and mammon). Luke's "sermon on a level place" is very like, and unlike, Matthew's "sermon on the mount" (Luke 6:17-49, Matt 5–7). Luke 13:10, 18-20 is set in a synagogue; Matt. 13:31-33 (the same utterance) is set by the sea. Matthew's account of the parable of the *talents* retains the colossal sums entrusted to his servants by the departing lord, but Luke speaks of far smaller sums of *pounds,* perhaps more intelligible to Gentiles — while retaining the story's message (Matt. 25:14ff., Luke 19:12ff.). But here something more has happened. Luke says that the lord was departing to "receive kingly power" and that some citizens sent after him a plea that it be refused; when he returned, he had those enemies executed. This adds nothing to the purpose of the story. The strange thing is that this is exactly what happened when Archelaus went to Rome after the death of his father, Herod, in 4 BC to be confirmed as ruler of part of his father's kingdom. It is not impossible that Jesus alluded to this, making the parable topical, but that fifty years later Matthew thought better to omit it. Or that during the repeated retelling of the parable this detail was added to the form which reached Luke, but not to that which reached Matthew. We merely guess: the puzzle illustrates the process by which memories of Jesus passed through many minds before becoming Gospels.

Something similar has happened to the straightforward parable that Luke (this time) records and Matthew elaborates. A fatuous remark by a fellow-diner, "Blessed is he who shall eat bread in the kingdom of God," evokes Jesus' response describing the actual situation as he knew it to be. "A great banquet," many invited; when all was ready, a string of empty excuses by the guests, servants sent into the highways to gather the poor and afflicted, the intended guests excluded (Luke 14:15ff.). Matthew (22:1-10) makes the banquet a marriage feast for a king's son, doubles the times the servants are sent to summon the invited, and adds that intended guests killed the servants. The king "destroyed those murderers" and "burned their city" before gathering new guests, "bad and good," from the thoroughfares. On seeing a guest ill-dressed, the king had him bound hand and foot and thrown out: "For many are called, but few are chosen." The military operations between the preparing of the meal, now "ready," and the finding of new guests sounds most implausible, even in a story; and the harshness towards an ill-dressed guest brought in unexpectedly from the streets is most unfair. The parable has surely developed in the frequent retelling. Perhaps another parable (of which only the last words survive) has become confused with Luke's straightforward one; just possibly, the ill-treatment of the servants and the burning of the invited guests' city reflect Jewish persecution of Christians and the destruction of Jerusalem (in 70 AD) added as a fitting embellishment of the original. More probably the punishment of a guest at God's table unworthy to be there may well be a fragment of another saying of Jesus on another occasion.

Other passages where the movement of thought is obscure and which may well be due to isolated sayings becoming connected by means of keywords or similarity of subject, to aid memory, are: Mark 9:47-50; Luke's sudden change of thought at 5:39 (compare Matt. 9:17); Matt. 18:1-14 (keyword "child"); Matthew 24 and 25 (Jesus' sayings on the future, near and far); Luke 9:57ff.; Mark 11:24-25. The parable of the embezzling steward seems complete at Luke 16:9 if we understand the permissive commendation of wealth as a mark of the wisdom commended in v. 8; vv. 10-13 appear to be comments obscuring the parable, probably sayings of Jesus (v. 13 = Matt 6:24) but not originally in this place. Some think that Mark 4:10-20, "explaining" the parable of the sower, has been influenced by the church's later experience more than Luke's crisper version (8:11-15). The same may be true of Matt. 13:36-43; the need to be patient in a church containing "evil-doers" seems again to reflect later experience.

Much of this is speculative. Where we can compare different Gospels and see what additions and alterations occur, we may feel more sure that years of repetition have left their mark. The chief value of these suggestions is to remind us how the words and deeds of Jesus came down to us. In view of the numerous factors influencing the transmission of these memories, it is not the variations that should surprise us, but the remarkable coherence of the resulting joint testimony. Prodigious memories, intense loyalty to Jesus, and the Spirit's guidance ensured that the total picture is authentic.

3

Figurative Language

THE MAIN DIFFERENCE between Jesus' language and our own is his constant use of visual metaphors. "Pictures fill his speech" to linger in our minds. This figurative style is no mere decoration: the language of Israel had few if any abstract nouns, "potentiality," "magnanimity," "nationhood," and the like. The psalmist did not speak of God's unfailing sustenance and rehabilitation, his supervision and hospitality. He said, "The LORD is my shepherd, I shall not want; he makes me lie down. . . . He leads me . . ." and prepares "a table before me . . ." Elsewhere the psalmist, speaking of God's protection, pictures himself creeping "under the shelter of [God's] wings" and calls God a strong tower, a rock, and a refuge. Ezekiel does not discuss transmissible culpability; instead, he says, "The fathers have eaten sour grapes, and the children's teeth are set on edge."

So Jesus calls God "Father," by one word ascribing to "the Most High" (the philosophers' "First Cause") personality, character, relationship, and goodwill.

Jesus adds that the divine goodwill is omniscient, particularized, dependable, insightful, and eternal. Or, as Jesus actually expresses it, God knows when even common sparrows fall; numbers the hairs of our heads; outdoes the carefulness of human fathers who would never give to children stones for bread, or a scorpion for an egg; needs not to be endlessly begged for favors, since he knows our needs; and in the end will welcome us to his house of many rooms. John would say it all in one abstract noun — "God is love" — but leave no picture on the mind.

With some daring, Jesus took up the commonest figure of speech in Jewish thought and transformed it. His kingdom is mentioned in the Gospels at least ninety-seven times, not once meaning literally a territory, population, and constitution such as most Jews expected the Messiah to restore. Asked when the kingdom of God was coming, Jesus answered, "The kingdom of God is not coming with signs to be observed . . . ;[it] is in the midst of you" (RSV; "within you," NIV; Luke's word is ambiguous). Jesus' kingdom is "hidden" (like leaven in dough, seed growing secretly, treasure in a field, a precious pearl in a jeweler's stock). To be in God's kingdom is to live under divine rule, to nurture a moral attitude; those who so live are the salt of the earth (purifying, preserving), the light of the world (illuminating, exposing), and leaven (stimulating all good in society).

By such influence the kingdom-people bear "fruit" to God, as branches in the sacred vine God planted in the world. One enters this kingdom by the strait gate of repentance and faith, the narrow way that leads to life. Jesus mentions too the keys of the kingdom, especially the key of knowledge which Jewish lawyers withhold, and he says the kingdom is for the childlike, requiring one to be born again. At the end, members of the kingdom will "sit at table" together, and the righteous will "shine like the sun."

Here are seventeen figures of speech on one subject. If we translate this teaching into philosophic terms it becomes very vague indeed, but generations of unsophisticated readers have understood Jesus' meaning very well. Jesus uses another twenty-five such figures to describe himself. More general, but no less striking, metaphors include:

For Jesus' coming ordeal, a "baptism" of "fire."
For his teaching, contrasted with repressive Judaism, "My yoke is easy, my burden is light."

For the impossibility of confining new truth and inspiration within old rules and rituals, "No one puts new wine into old wineskins. . . . new wine will burst the skins, and they and the wine be lost."

"No one sews a piece of unshrunk cloth on an old garment . . . the new tears the old . . . a worse tear is made."

For his gift of new, refreshing life and thought, "living water" (not from old and stagnant wells like Jacob's, and like Judaism).

"If I do not wash you, you have no part with me" — feet-washing symbolizing deeper purification.

"He who believes in me, out of his heart shall flow rivers of living water" into other lives.

For evangelists and their work: "fishers of men . . . catching men."

For the difference between those who hear and obey, and those who hear and ignore, two houses beset by storm, one surviving, the other destroyed.

For the fickleness of his generation, rejecting the Baptist for his austerity and Jesus for his sociability, children complaining "we piped . . . and you did not dance, we wailed at funerals, and you did not weep."

For the wealthy man planning greater barns, "not rich toward God . . . no treasure in heaven."

For the last judgment, "separating sheep from goats" (in Palestine the two are almost indistinguishable).

When ordered to silence singing children, the stones would cry out . . . "out of the mouths of babes and sucklings . . . perfect praise."

So fertile and spontaneous was Jesus' picture-language inventiveness that we cannot hope to understand him until we grow used to this visual presentation of truth. It may help if we recall that "the common people heard him gladly." This was partly because he spoke as they did

— his images were drawn from their daily experience as "country people," field-workers, fisherfolk, housewives, shepherds. Cities were few,
urban life not far removed from the surrounding fields or seashore,
and Jerusalem was often full of country pilgrims. And he himself was a
villager and a man of his hands.

So his word-pictures tend to become elaborate. The metaphor of
"seed," Christ's word in the parable of the sower where Jesus analyzes
the varied results of his Galilean ministry (and everyone with field or
garden would recognize those soil conditions!), recurs in "one sows,
another reaps"; "that sower and reaper may rejoice together"; the phe-
nomenal growth of mustard seed; the seed (of the kingdom) growing
secretly; the good seed in the world's soil are the "sons of the kingdom"; he himself must fall into the ground and die as does a seed, that
there might be a harvest.

That important idea of harvest, upon which survival itself might
depend, also recurs. Peter is to be sifted by Satan, as newly gathered
wheat is sifted before use; harvesting needs laborers at morning, mid-
day, and evening; good and bad must grow together until harvest,
when the difference is clearer; when the fields are white, men should
pray "the Lord of the harvest" for more laborers; there will be no harvest worth reaping if the plowman keeps looking backward; moreover,
let self-appointed leaders never forget that "Every plant which my
heavenly Father has not planted will be rooted up."

The figure of the shepherd influenced Israel's thought from the
days of the shepherds Abraham and Jacob to the one-time shepherd
and psalmist David. Ezekiel blamed Judah's ruling "shepherds" for her
disasters and promised that God himself would be her shepherd
henceforth. It was therefore still a living metaphor when Jesus saw the
leaderless, untutored crowds as sheep without a shepherd, "harassed
and helpless," and sent his disciples to "the lost sheep of the house of
Israel." His claim to be "the good shepherd," giving his life to protect
the sheep; his story of the seeking shepherd; his warning that if the
shepherd is smitten the sheep would be scattered; that he sends his disciples as sheep among wolves; and the promise that he would gather

"other sheep" not of Judah's fold: all this had weight in Jewish minds that it cannot have for city dwellers. So too his remark that it is those who do not belong to his sheep who do not believe in him, while his sheep hear his voice, and he knows them; they shall never perish, nor be snatched from his — or his Father's — hands.

The lack of efficient lighting for homes and streets created serious problems; as Jesus observed, "If anyone walks in the day he does not stumble, because he sees the light of this world. But if anyone walks in the night he stumbles, because the light is not in him." Life so governed by daylight is unknown to most modern people, who therefore miss the relevance of the promise, by Jesus "the light of the world," that "he who follows me shall not walk in darkness, but will have the light of life" — meaning especially mental and moral illumination, implying also hope and comfort for dark times. Until the coming of Jesus, the Gentiles were said to "sit in darkness"; Jesus announced, "As long as I am in the world, I am the light of the world," and the implied warning is repeated later: "The light is with you for a little longer. Walk while you have the light, lest the darkness overtake you; he who walks in the darkness does not know where he goes. While you have the light, believe in the light, that you may become sons of light." One last echo of the same warning: "I have come as light into the world, that whoever believes in me may not remain in darkness."

The light metaphor also yields clear lessons for disciples. "You are the light of the world. A city set on a hill cannot be hid. Nor do men light a lamp and put it under a bushel, but on a stand, and it gives light to all in the house. Let your light so shine before men" (be shining examples). Using another image, Jesus warns, "The eye is the lamp of the body. So, if your eye is sound, your whole body will be full of light; but if your eye is not sound, your whole body will be full of darkness. If then the light in you is darkness, how great is the darkness!" Or, as Luke completes the saying, "Be careful lest the light in you" (what you think is light) "be darkness." Jesus evidently has in mind the effect of prejudice, false assumptions, and self-interest clouding the mind and conscience, effectively dimming or wholly obscuring the light he offers. Darkness, after all, may be due to blindness as well as to nightfall; it is possible to remain willfully in darkness. Only the totally honest, teachable, courageous, and selfless mind can see truth clearly, and make earnest disciples into "sons of light."

Two thousand years of repetition in sermons, hymns, prayers, and public and private reading have robbed Christ's figurative language of some of its freshness and surprise. These few examples show how worthwhile it is to try to recapture the background and the relevance of his metaphors, and to read them as if for the first time, and with imagination.

4

Missing the Point

O F COURSE the prosaic, unimaginative literalism of many Western minds can make fun of Jesus' picture-language. Nothing is easier. Jesus said there are no marriages in heaven, yet the heavenly Father has a son! If God is Father of all, then all are brothers and sisters, and there should be no marriages on earth. If God sees the sparrow fall, why does he not catch it, or teach it to nest on the ground?

This sort of argumentation is not as ridiculous as it sounds. Much ink has been spilled over Jesus' saying that he came to give his life "a ransom" for many. To whom was the ransom paid — to God? Is then God so jealous of his rights as to demand his son's death to set men free? To the devil, then? But has the devil any rights at all? An old, old puzzle. If the saved can look back gratefully to the grace that saved and kept them, knowing it was all of God's good will, not their own effort, then the thousands of unsaved must have been abandoned — predestined — to remain unsaved and to go to hell.

All this kind of logomachy — which simply means a dispute about words — results from arguing from the literal words of the metaphors and not from their meaning. It is shallow intellectualism, missing the point — Jesus' point — by treating the illustration as a principle or premise and drawing conclusions from that. It is foolish — and it can also be cruel, as when it consigns multitudes to damnation on account of a phrase, or when it resorts to torture, rack, and stake to extort a particular formulation of words.

But prosaic literalism can impoverish our understanding of Jesus in less dramatic ways. It is a pity, for example, to miss the occasional humor in Jesus' words just because we assume he was always deadly serious. When Jesus compared the wild lilies that clothed the plain of Esdraelon with "Solomon in all his glory," did no one smile? When he spoke of the rich man struggling to enter God's kingdom like a camel wriggling through the eye of a needle, did no one in the company guffaw? (Too sober scholars want to change it to "cable," as if that eased the comparison; or to a small door in the city gate — solemnly missing the fun.) Or again, when he described the Pharisee carefully counting the stems of the smallest three herbs in his garden in order to give exactly "the tithe of all his produce" to the Lord, did no one chuckle? Or when the same Pharisee scrubbed and rubbed and carefully dried the outside of his cup, according to the law — and forgot to clean the inside!

To advise Jews not to be too concerned about clothes, food, or wealth, because after these things "the Gentiles seek," would elicit a wry grin in some quarters. And his picture of the strutting religious leaders, shouldering their way through the marketplace, nodding "Morning, Father . . ." here, "Good day, Rabbi . . ." there, their long cape tassels swinging, their scripture-boxes fastened on wrist and brow with the broadest ribbons, the same leaders who were always in the forefront at feasts and occupying the prominent seats in synagogue: there was serious purpose in the caricature, but Jesus knew some hearers would repeat the phrases to each other with sly enjoyment.

The picture-in-words that would most often be repeated with amusement is that hilarious snapshot of the Pharisee taking refreshment in the sunshine. Lifting his cup to his lips he starts suddenly — a fly has settled on his drink, an "unclean" morsel in the strict Rabbinic code. So he pauses, lifts the fringe of his cape, draws it gently over the surface of the liquid to eliminate the offending mite, and swallows his drink. And next, Jesus says, he proceeds to swallow — a camel! "The long hairy neck, all that amplitude of loose-hung anatomy, the hump, two humps, both of them slid down . . and the legs, all of them, with the whole outfit of knobby knees and big padded feet — the Pharisee swallows a camel and never notices!" (T. R. Glover).

Certainly the meaning is serious, and very sharp, for Jesus charged the Pharisee class with a hopelessly disproportionate sense of moral and religious duty, meticulous about ritual trifles, wholly blind to "weightier matters" like mercy, compassion, truth, and humility. But the listening crowd would not need an explanation; like all good caricatures, the picture speaks for itself, and the phrase "straining at a gnat and swallowing a camel" has become part of the English language.

These examples of Jesus' humor touch also upon his skillful use of irony. Jesus had no need to mention the camels or the Gentiles to make his point, but bringing them in sharpens his point, adding a touch of criticism or satire. It is present again in his asking whether the crowds went out to see the Baptist expecting to see a prince in soft clothing, or a reed shaken by the wind. When disciples quarrel about who will be first in the kingdom, Jesus likens them to ambitious rival kings contending for territory — but adds that such kings call themselves "Benefactors" of their people. That word has a sting, for it is the term used on ancient coins — denoting rulers who were rarely benefactors. Irony sharpens the remark Jesus made to those who came to arrest him: "When I was with you day after day in the Temple you did not lay hands on me. But this" — secretly, by night, in the deserted garden — "this is your hour, and the power of darkness." The occasion fits the deed, and the doers.

Sharpest irony of all, perhaps, is Jesus' stern comment: "It cannot be that a prophet shall perish away from Jerusalem." It is hardly possible to miss the point of that.

On two occasions at least this ironical note may be the true explanation of puzzling incidents. Peter reported to Jesus that tax collectors had come, asking if the Master paid the lawful dues. Jesus appears to assert his freedom from the tax, as the son of a king, but adds,

"However, not to give offense to them, go to the sea and cast a hook, and take the first fish that comes up, and when you open its mouth you will find a shekel; take that and give it to them for me and for yourself." Two questions arise. Is this a "Christian" way to pay one's debts, relying on a fortuitous sort of miracle to provide the resources to meet one's responsibilities? Or is Jesus simply "teasing" Peter, so troubled about the cash? Is Jesus simply saying, "Peter, Peter, you a fisherman! There's the sea! Do I have to tell *you* how to earn a shekel?"

The other puzzling incident follows the refusal of a wealthy young inquirer to sell all and follow Jesus. Remembering the boats and nets and fishing business at home, Peter blurts out, "Lo, we have left everything and followed you. What then shall we have?" Jesus answers (according to Matthew): "Truly, I say to you, in the new world, when the Son of man shall sit on his glorious throne, you . . . will also sit on twelve thrones, judging the twelve tribes of Israel. And every one who has left houses or brothers or sisters or father or mother or children or lands, for my name's sake, will receive a hundredfold, and inherit eternal life." Matthew and Mark have the solemn warning (to all disciples) "But many that are first will be last, and the last first."

Mark and Luke leave out Peter's outrageous question. Mark omits the twelve thrones judging the twelve tribes, but instead of "in the new world, when the Son of man shall sit on his glorious throne" he places the bountiful future "now in this time," although "with persecutions," and "in the age to come, eternal life." Astonishingly, Mark has Jesus promising "now in this time" a hundredfold houses, brothers, sisters, mothers, children, and lands.

These variations are evidence that the evangelists (or the eyewitnesses who reported the saying) felt some difficulty with it, not surprisingly. "Twelve thrones" would include a throne for Judas, who the evangelists know by now has betrayed Jesus. And what would these men do with hundreds of houses — or, for that matter, with hundreds of children? The twelve tribes, moreover, had by Jesus' time been greatly reduced — to say the least. And the confusion as to time, whether "in the new world" or "in this time," is significant, as is the sobering addition of "persecutions." Beyond all this, it is very difficult to believe that Jesus promised wholesale material, domestic, and social rewards to all who follow him. Subsequent history falsifies any such idea — as do Jesus' other warnings of persecution, imprisonment, and martyrdom.

It is a relief to turn to Luke's version. He abbreviates and generalizes, almost "spiritualizes," the promise: "There is no man who has left [all] who will not receive manifold more in this time, and in the age to come eternal life." Surely Luke has the essence of the reply to Peter. But whence came the other versions? The simplest explanation seems to be that Jesus responded to Peter with ironic exaggeration: "Oh, you people will one day have all that you have ever dreamed of, and much, much more, don't worry." Was Peter's face red?

Some imagine it irreverent to look behind Jesus' use of words in this way to discover his real meaning. Yet could Jesus have meant literally his counsel to his disciples, "Let him who has no sword sell his mantle and buy one"? Certainly not, because when the disciples, taking the words literally, answered, "Look, Lord, here are two swords," Jesus dismissed them in exasperation with "Enough of that" (literal Greek "It is enough," not "they are" or "two are" enough). Later again, Jesus assured Pilate, "My kingship is not of this world. . . . [If it were] . . . my servants would fight. . . ." To misread Jesus in either case, taking the words literally, not merely misses the point but seriously misrepresents his whole attitude toward arms.

Similarly, Jesus cannot have meant literally the advice recorded in Matthew and Mark, "If your hand or your foot causes you to sin, cut it off and throw it from you. . . . If your eye causes you to sin, pluck it out. . . ." Jesus surely was not asking his followers to practice self-mutilation. Significantly, though Luke preserves the opening words of this counsel, "Temptations to sin are sure to come . . . ," he does not go on to record these almost ruthless commands. Jesus' words in Matthew and Mark stress with his usual visual vigor the extreme seriousness of sin. To focus on the harsh language alone must not become an excuse for missing his point — as it often does.

Much the same must be said of the words "Whoever causes one

of these little ones who believe in me to sin, it would be better for him to have a great millstone fastened round his neck and to be drowned in the depth of the sea." Jesus could startle sometimes; but the forcefulness of the words reflects only the depth of his righteous indignation at the callousness with which some would lead the immature astray. Jesus does not intend that society should in fact drown such people. He says only, "It would be better for him . . ."; perhaps he was thinking of the even sterner judgment of God.

When one man offers to follow Jesus anywhere, Jesus warns of the cost; when another asks time to say farewell to his family, Jesus warns against looking backward; and when a third desires first to bury his father, Jesus answers, "Leave the dead to bury their own dead; but as for you, go and proclaim the kingdom." All three sayings sternly assert the priority of God's kingdom over all other claims: that is Jesus' point. Impulsive, ill-considered offers to follow, prevaricating delay for a family party, or waiting for a father to die will not do. (If the father were already dead, the man would not be chatting to Jesus but arranging the necessary same-day funeral.) As elsewhere, Jesus demands that we "seek *first* the kingdom. . . ." As he did himself.

Once we grasp the fact that, though Jesus must always be taken seriously, he did not always speak with literal exactness, certain other possibilities arise which may be helpful. We begin to wonder, for example, whether the story of Christ's temptation, which could only have come from his lips, is to be taken literally or as a very real experience described in figurative language. Luke's record suggests the temptations continued until later, and the kinds of tests — to win a kingdom by beneficent miracles, by wonders and signs, or by the devil's own methods — are precisely the alternative ways to power that confronted Jesus throughout his ministry and that he repeatedly rejected. If there is anything to this suggestion that Jesus laid bare his inner experience in figurative terms, we are relieved from bewilderment at the prospect of the devil's quoting Scripture or of Jesus' being lifted bodily by demonic power to the temple roof miles away. We cannot dogmatize on such a possibility, but . . .

It is equally possible — no more — that Jesus' congratulation of the Twelve on the report of their mission, "I saw Satan fall like lightning from heaven," should be understood not as literal description but as a picturesque expression of triumph. And that "creepy story" (as it has been called) of the exorcised soul repossessed by an evil spirit and seven others more evil may also be a powerful metaphor. Its warning of the dangers, spiritual and psychological, of a merely negative religion and an empty life would remain.

There is one other mistaken literalism that can distort interpretation, ignoring the tendency of figurative language to exaggerate. English abounds with common phrases which exaggerate, sometimes wildly, for the sake of emphasis: "*mountain*ous seas," "over*kill*," "*murder*ous glance," "looking like a *million dollars*," or "*volcanic* temper." No one takes such exaggeration seriously. So Jesus could mention seed in a good soil bringing forth fruit "an hundredfold," and scholars solemnly debate whether ancient seed in arid eastern soil could ever produce more than thirty- to fortyfold. The promise about treading on serpents and scorpions, the requirement to forgive a repenting brother four hundred and ninety times, the grain of mustard that has birds singing in its eventual branches — all should surely be treated as figurative exaggerations. So should the promise that faith as a grain of mustard seed could say to this sycamine tree "be rooted up and be planted in the sea," and it would obey.

Figurative exaggeration for emphasis is a valid device of rhetoric. This is not, however, a convenient argument to be used to tone down every challenging word or extravagant promise of Jesus. He did very often startle dull minds and stab sleeping consciences with the vastness of his claims, demands, and certainties. And we must take his words, if not in every instance literally, always seriously.

5

Parables and Other Devices

JESUS' FAMOUS PARABLES are in effect extended metaphors, a figure of speech suggesting likeness or analogy. As Israel's language avoided abstract terms, so her method of teaching avoided abstract religious and moral messages, but rather told stories to illustrate them. Jotham's parable of the trees seeking a king, Nathan's parable of the traveler demanding the poor man's lamb, and similar figurative lessons by the wise woman of Tekoa, Ezekiel, and Isaiah would all be familiar to Jesus from his school and synagogue days.

Certainly Jesus excelled at this method of fastening deep thoughts upon nonreading minds. The Gospels record more than forty of his parables, from a simple story like "The kingdom of heaven is like leaven which a woman took and hid in three measures of meal till it was all leavened" to a complex story that in fact reviewed Jewish history and forecast total change — the parable of the vineyard. Some of the parables *compare* God (or Christ himself) to a familiar character (a careful father, a seeking shepherd), and others *contrast* God with known characters (an unjust judge, a churlish neighbor). Others liken spiritual processes to natural ones (seed-sowing, the barren tree) or attach spiritual lessons to everyday situations that will later recall those lessons to mind (the two houses, the wheat and the weeds).

Usually, each parable makes one main point. To draw out minor lessons from the details may sometimes have some interest, even some value; but it is essential to distinguish the Lord's main point from whatever else we find in the story. Three parables — the lost sheep, the lost coin, and the prodigal son — illustrate the joy of heaven in finding what has been lost. It is not certain that the three were spoken together, though each is appropriate to the situation in which Luke sets them, the criticism of Christ's friendship with sinners. But we can see that three ways of getting lost happen to be illustrated — stupidity, neglect, or willfulness — and also three ways of being saved: being carried home, being discovered, or having to trudge all the way along. In the prodigal's story, Jesus himself draws a second lesson in answer to his critics, likening them to an elder brother who resents the prodigal's return.

Nevertheless *our* ingenuity must never be allowed to distort Christ's meaning, which the occasion of his speaking often defines for us. Nor may we turn his illustration of one truth into a "proof" of another. Some have argued that "there is no Christ in the prodigal's story," concluding there is no need for a Savior. This is to ignore the obvious truth that only Jesus could tell such a story with divine authority; no one had ever so represented God before.

Truth must stand on its own feet before it can be illustrated anywhere. The parable of the foolish bridesmaids does *not* prove that half the women in the world are improvident; nor does the parable of Dives and Lazarus prove long-distance communication between heaven and hell.

To claim freedom in applying Jesus' stories prompts a special caution. Jesus took illustrations from the world as it was, without in the least implying that he approved of the way the world did things. He admired the cleverness of the embezzling steward without condoning the use he made of it. Jesus described the vineyard owner's generous payment to those who came late in the day to work — and his assertion of his right to do what he would with his own — without thereby defining a fair wage policy or defending the use of wealth without social responsibility. Jesus was neither economist nor politician. Nor does Jesus imply that the prodigal's behavior was the sure way for youth to gain a father's attention, or that "finding is keeping" when treasure turns up in a field. We may not assume that Jesus would approve of the waste of sowing seed on rocky places, along footpaths, and among thorns. The callous indifference of the unjust judge toward a widow in distress would certainly earn his condemnation.

In all such illustrations, drawn from situations his hearers would recognize, it was enough to indicate the similarity or the contrast with some spiritual truth in a single point, without adding a paragraph of moral valuation of human behavior.

> *The two houses* emphasizes obedience above knowledge, and the impartiality of life's storms.
>
> *The weeds, the dragnet* demand that judgment of others be left to God and time.
>
> *The treasure discovered, the pearl sought out* show the priceless value and quiet beauty of life under God's rule.
>
> *The leaven, the mustard seed* are optimistic about the kingdom's inherent power — beyond all expectation.
>
> *The seed growing secretly* stresses the unostentatious progress of truth and spiritual power.
>
> *The importuning neighbor, the unjust judge* urge persistence in prayer.
>
> *The embezzling steward* teaches the need of intelligence in piety.
>
> *The sons' yes and no, the pharisee and the publican* both emphasize that truth is more important than profession.
>
> *The two debtors* (which loves most?), *the two debtors* (one forgiven but not forgiving) stress the obligations involved in divine mercy.
>
> *The good Samaritan* shows a foreigner answering both "Who is my neighbor?" and "What is love?"
>
> *The rich fool, Dives and Lazarus* both contrast earthly with divine wealth in the light of the outcome.

The tower, the war both deprecate impulsive discipleship.

The ten bridesmaids, the shut door stress that readiness is all.

The Master leaving (a) *investments,* (b) *fellow servants,* or (c) *watchfulness* provides lessons for the coming time of Jesus' departure.

The laborers in the vineyard tells that to serve at all is a privilege, and rewards are God's to adjudge.

The tenants of the vineyard (Jesus' comment on Isaiah 5) foresees Christ's rejection and the giving of the kingdom to other believers.

The barren tree stresses the divine patience.

The vine teaches that the condition of fruitfulness is abiding.

The marriage feast shows invited guests refusing, so outsiders are welcomed.

The wedding garment (an appended fragment?) demonstrates that admission is free, but worthiness remains an obligation once inside.

The sheep and goats promise the universal and mainly ethical basis of final judgment.

The fig tree urges that we live in watchful expectation.

The word "parable" does, however, have other meanings. In Luke 6:39 it means a question or series of questions — "Can a blind man lead a blind man? . . . Why do you see the speck that is in your brother's eye, but do not notice the log that is in your own eye?" The questions still imply some *comparison,* that of the "unseeing" disciple with literal blindness and with self-righteousness blind to its own faults. The parables of the tower and the king going to war (Luke 14:28ff.) don't tell a story, but both again make a basic comparison between ill-advised builders and kings, embarking on impossible ventures, and would-be disciples. In Matthew 15:15, "parable" is used of a difficult saying which Peter wants explained. This is how the word is used in the Greek Old Testament at Psalm 49:4 ("riddle") and Psalm 78:2, parallel to "dark sayings"; and again, as requiring mental alertness and right judgment, in Proverbs 1:6 ("riddles") and 26:7, 9, translated "proverb" which fools cannot understand. This meaning — riddle, dark saying — offers some help in understanding Mark 4:10-12, where "parables" appear to be used to *hide* truth from the outsider. No one has satisfactorily explained this. But perhaps in verse 10 "parable" is used in the sense of "riddle." To grasp religious truth does require a mind and heart willing to learn. To the careless and unbelieving, much even in Jesus' teaching amounts to mysterious sayings and "religious riddles," until teachable faith makes things clear.

The Old Testament familiarized Jews not only with spoken parables but with acted ones. Jeremiah purchased and wore a noticeably new loincloth, traveled to Babylon to hide it, then later retrieved it and exhibited it spoiled, signifying how God would spoil Judah's pride. He bought an earthenware flask and while preaching in the iniquitous Valley of Hinnom smashed it to pieces. In the same significant way he bore for days a heavy yoke and later bought a field in the possession of the enemy. Ezekiel made a model of the city upon a rooftile and flung it in pieces; Hosea gave unusual names to his children — all public performances which set the onlookers arguing about what these odd antics meant.

So Jesus spread clay upon a blind man's eyes and sent him groping through the city streets to the pool of Siloam, followed by a gaping crowd. When he washed and (as he said) "came seeing," a long argument ensued until Jesus explained that he had come that the blind might see. Jesus left a fig tree outside the city gates standing fruitless and withered. Until then year after year passing pilgrims expected to pick a fig or two; it said all Jesus felt about a nation bearing for God nothing but leaves. Thus also he rose in silence from supper, laid aside his garments, girded himself with a towel, and knelt before each of his men in turn, washing their feet: a heartbreaking rebuke to their quarreling about precedence, and an unforgettable example.

When he arranged for a donkey to be ready at the approach to the feast day and rode among the pilgrims from Galilee in the way a prophet said their king would come, no one needed telling what he meant. The raising of Lazarus shows the same careful timing for maximum effect — and the Jewish Council met at once to decide what to do with him. And when he took a small child into the crook of his arm and spoke of how adults must receive the kingdom, those present would long remember the scene as well as the words.

Such actions-plus-meaning are not, of course, "parables," but they illustrate again the love of the figurative presentation of truth with which we of the West must come to terms if we would appreciate Jesus' teaching as we ought.

Other features of Jesus' speech to watch for include a liking for antitheses, setting good and bad, false and true, example and warning in opposition:

Pharisee and publican
God seeing in secret, rewarding openly
Son said "Yes," son said "No"
Faithful in least, in much
God and mammon
Treasure on earth, in heaven
Two debtors (used twice)
Right hand, left hand
Wise and foolish bridesmaids
Serpents and doves
Lambs and wolves
Broad and narrow way

It is easy to find thirty or more of these. Such a habit of speech greatly assisted hearers' memories. So did Jesus' fondness for pithy proverbs:

The first shall be last, the last first.
With God all things are possible.
Many are called but few are chosen.
The kingdom of God is within you.
If you know, . . . happy are you if you do.
Sufficient unto the day is the evil thereof.

Remember Lot's wife.
Out of the overflow of the heart the mouth speaks.
The spirit is willing, the flesh weak.
Wisdom is justified by all her children.

Again examples could be multiplied. And of course there are many instances of profound things very simply said:

"Where two or three are gathered in my name, there am I in the
  midst of them."
"This is the work of God, that you believe in him whom he has
  sent."
"Where your treasure is, there will your heart be also."
"It is your Father's good pleasure to give you the kingdom."
"By this all men will know that you are my disciples, if you have
  love for one another."
"If any man would come after me, let him deny himself and take
  up his cross and follow me."

No one can honestly hide behind the excuse that he cannot understand Jesus.

"Sense and sanity are the marks of Jesus' religion," says one well-informed commentator. "Where did this man get this wisdom?" was an inquiry raised in Jesus' home district. Jews were familiar with the sage with books of proverbs and wisdom for the guidance of everyday life, and it is worth noting that Jesus, too, was so consulted, his impartiality, insight, and good sense making his counsel valuable even on nonreligious topics.

Thus he was asked to settle a dispute about inheritance, which he refused to do, being no arbitrator. Observing guests maneuvering for seats at the "top table," Jesus remarks that it is wiser to take lower seats and be invited higher than to take higher seats and be told to move down: there is social wisdom in humility. He advises litigants to compromise before going to court — it's cheaper. He quotes (apparently) a familiar proverb about pearls thrown to swine, to urge discrimination before entering into religious arguments with people desiring only to debate.

Foresight of others' feelings lies behind the counsel to traveling missioners to accept, and to stay with, the first hospitality offered them, not to move to richer houses when "fame" creates the opportunity. Experience prompts the warning that nothing is so secret that it will not sometimes become known. Very perceptive, too, in an "occupied" country is the advice that, when commandeered to walk a mile carrying military baggage, it is better to offer to go further, voluntarily, than to resent every step with bitterness of soul. And equally shrewd is the counsel that, since worrying will not add to your height or change the color of a hair, what's the point of worrying?

It is not surprising that sometimes people sought Jesus' opinion on current events like the fall of a tower, the threats of Herod, the violence of Pilate, the moral puzzle of a baby being born blind, rival miracle workers. And it is very significant to note how often Jesus refused to speculate, to argue merely theoretic questions, or to "explain" theological puzzles. Sometimes he turned questions to good account: "You repent, never mind other people's sins!" And if occasionally he was warned of danger to himself, he merely affirmed the divine plan of his career, and continued his mission with calm courage.

"Sense and sanity," certainly, based upon courage and faith made Jesus a wise counselor, a dependable friend; in this as in so many things the example of intelligent and enduring piety.

6

The Questioning Christ: Authority

JESUS ASKED two hundred twelve questions — that is, so far as dupli-
cate records, slightly varying forms, or questions in one Gospel that
occasionally appear as statements in another enable one to count accu-
rately. Obviously, inquiry was as important a feature of his teaching
method as metaphors and parables. He conveyed truth in conversation
more than in sermons and never in lectures. The great Greek teacher
Socrates used relentless interrogation to expose ignorance; so did Jesus,
where ignorance was to be blamed, as in over-confident lawyers,
priests, and Pharisees. More often Jesus questioned to define needs,
search hearts, reveal motives, prompt insight, or simply to elicit facts.
His most trenchant use of questions, though, was in countering arguments, often with devastating effect. Often a pertinent question conveyed his point — unanswerably.

At least nine of Jesus' questions seek information, such as "How
many loaves have you?"; "Do you see anything?" (while healing blindness); "Who do men say that the Son of man is?"; "Where have you
laid him?" (Lazarus). There is not the slightest evidence that these
were pretended inquiries, that Jesus knew the answers before he asked.
That would imply something near deceit. And Jesus was really man,
truly incarnate, not masquerading as human. Nor was his sadness

feigned in "When the Son of man comes, will he find faith on earth?" or in "Will you also go away?"

To illustrate Jesus' use of interrogation, only a selection need be given, representing:

a. **Questions that opened a relationship:**
"What do you seek?" to John's two disciples.
"What is your name?" to the insane man at Gadara.
"Do you want to be healed?" to the paralyzed at Bethzatha.
"Because I said I saw you under the fig tree, do you believe?" to Nathanael.
"O woman, what have you to do with me?" to his mother, signaling the new relationship created by his leaving home and by his mission.

b. **Questions that ask the opinion of the hearer:**
"What do you think? If a man has a hundred sheep, and one of them has gone astray, does he not leave the ninety and nine . . . ?"
"What do you think, Simon? From whom do kings . . . take toll or tribute?"
"Is a lamp brought in to be put under a bushel . . . not on a stand?"
"I ask you, is it lawful on the Sabbath to do good or to do harm?"
"Can a blind man lead a blind man?"
"Which of you, desiring to build a tower, does not first sit down and count the cost?"
"What do you think of the Christ? Whose son is he?"

In each instance (there are many) the answer spoken or assumed is the ground for the next utterance.

c. **Questions that sharpen Jesus' meaning by the hearers' agreement:**

"If you love those who love you, what reward have you? Do not even the tax collectors do the same?"

"Is not life more than food, and the body more than clothing?"

"Are you not of more value than [the birds]?"

"How can you say to your brother, 'Let me take the speck out of your eye,' when there is the log in your own eye?"

"What man of you, if his son asks him for a loaf, will give him a stone?"

d. **Questions that help people sort themselves out:**

"Why do you trouble the woman? She has done a beautiful thing."

"Will you lay down your life for me? . . . [You will deny me three times]."

"Woman, why are you weeping . . . Whom do you seek?" (Gentle invitations to unburden mind and heart.)

"Is this what you are asking yourselves, what I meant by saying, 'A little while, and you will not see me, and again . . . you will see me?'"

"What were you discussing on the way?"

"Friend, why are you here? . . . Would you betray the Son of man with a kiss?"

"Do you love me more than these?" (as Peter suggested he did).

"So, could you not watch with me one hour?"

e. **Questions that evoke better discipleship:**

"Why are you afraid? Have you no faith?"

"Why do you discuss . . . the fact that you have no bread? Do you not yet perceive . . . ?"

"Are your hearts hardened? . . . Do you not yet understand?"

"Have I been with you so long, and yet you do not know me, Philip?"

"What do you want? . . . Are you able to drink the cup that I am
to drink" (when James and John asked for privileges).

"Are you also still without understanding?"

"Do you know what I have done to you?" (after the feet washing).

"Why do you call me 'Lord, Lord,' and not do what I tell you?"

f. Questions that are unanswerable, innocent, and disarming:

"Will any one of you who has a servant . . . say to him when he
has come in from the field, 'Come at once and sit down at table'? . . . Does he thank the servant . . . ?" (on expecting rewards for duty done).

"Do you not say, 'There are yet four months, then comes the
harvest'? I tell you . . . the fields are already white."

"Shall I not drink the cup which the Father has given me?"

"What is the kingdom of God like? And to what shall I compare
it . . . ?"

"How can Satan cast out Satan?"

"Which is greater, the gift or the altar that makes the gift sacred?"

g. Questions that are armed and that are dangerous to answer:

"If I cast out demons by Beelzebub, by whom do your sons cast
them out?"

"Why do you transgress the commandments of God for the sake
of your tradition?"

"Does not each of you on the Sabbath untie his ox or his ass . . .
and lead it away to water it?"

"Of how much more value is a man than a sheep?"

"The baptism of John, whence was it? From heaven or from
men?" (Either answer would involve Jesus' critics in trouble,
for not responding to John, or for denying his prophetic authority. They say, "We do not know.")

h. **Questions that are weapons of controversy; Jesus makes a questioner commit himself to some fact or principle, and so answer his own question:**

"Why put me to the test? Show me a coin . . ."; "Whose likeness and inscription is this?" (They say "Caesar's" — a compromising reply!) "Render to Caesar what [you admit] belongs to him."

"Two debtors, one owing ten times what the other owes . . . both being forgiven, which of them will love the creditor most?" The hostile host admits, "He who is forgiven most." With that answer Jesus defended the sinful woman who had wept over his feet.

A lawyer asks, "Who is my neighbor?" Jesus answers with the parable of priest and levite passing an injured man, and a Samaritan attending to him devotedly, then asks the lawyer, "Which of these three, do you think, proved neighbor to the man who fell among the robbers?" The lawyer, not Jesus, answers the crucial question.

Challenged about his view on divorce, Jesus asks, "What did Moses command you?" then cites Moses in reply, from Genesis, showing their doctrine was wrong.

i. **Questions that challenge his opponents' ignorance, or mishandling, of their boasted Scriptures. Pharisees claimed to adhere strictly to every rule of the law; scribes were trained to copy, interpret, and teach the law; Sadducees accepted only the original Scriptures, the books of Moses. Jesus asked, in public:**

"Have you never read what David did, when he . . . was hungry, . . . how he . . . ate the bread of the Presence, which it is not lawful for any but the priests to eat?"

"Have you never read, 'Out of the mouth of babes . . . thou hast perfected praise'?"

"Have you never read . . . , 'The very stone which the builders rejected has become the head of the corner'?"

"Have you not read how on the Sabbath the priests in the Temple profane the Sabbath and are guiltless?"

"Have you not read that he who made them . . . male and female said, '. . . the two shall become one'?"

"Have you not read what was said to you by God, 'I am the God of Abraham, and the God of Isaac, and the God of Jacob'? He is not God of the dead but of the living?" (proving immortality to the Sadducees from their meager Bible).

"Is it not written, 'My house shall be called a house of prayer . . .'? But you have made it a den of robbers."

"Is not this why you are wrong, that you know neither the scriptures nor the power of God?"

A teaching method so persistent and so searching must rest upon an assumption central to Jesus' mission. That assumption is clearly expressed in the crucial question, "Why do you not judge for yourselves what is right?" This quite fundamental inquiry was addressed, not to religious leaders or educated lay people, but "to the multitudes" (Luke 12:54-57). And it was contrasted with their readiness to read the signs of coming rain or heat, but their unwillingness to interpret the time in which they lived. So Jesus takes for granted the common people's ability to "judge what is right" *when presented with the truth* and *when they were willing to acknowledge it.* To appreciate properly the fundamental significance of this assumption we must set beside it several of Jesus' utterances.

1. Jesus warns not to judge by appearances, but with "right judgment" (John 7:24).
2. He warns against letting "the light within" us become darkness (Luke 11:35, Matt. 6:23). It will be recalled that Jesus likens this to the darkness suffered by the whole body when the physical eye is unsound. So the willful closing of the inward eye to spiritual truth leaves the whole mind, soul, and spirit in darkness. Jesus says he has come to open such blind eyes — to awaken again the capacity to see what is true and of God.

3. Jesus' repeatedly demands, "Why does this generation seek for a sign?" — for some overwhelming cosmic manifestation to "prove" what they can perceive by their own reason and conscience to be true and manifestly of God. It is only a "wicked and adulterous" (unfaithful) "generation" that needs supernatural signs to convince them of what they are too spiritually blind to recognize as divine (Matt. 12:39, 16:4ff.). Therefore the only sign Jesus would promise was that of a prophet preaching truth. In any case, Jesus' critics themselves showed that miracles and signs did not guarantee spiritual truth, for without denying his miracles they confidently ascribed them to the power of Beelzebub. Such an accusation, Jesus declared, showed a *willful* inability to distinguish good from evil, which placed such accusers beyond the inner teaching of the Spirit, and thus beyond forgiveness (Matt. 12:24ff.). In them the inner light had indeed given place to darkness.

4. Jesus suggests why it is that, having the intellectual and moral capacity to recognize the truth, so many fail to do so. At one point he cites Isaiah's explanation: "seeing they do not see, and hearing they do not hear, nor do they understand. With them indeed is fulfilled the prophecy of Isaiah which says:

> 'You shall indeed hear but never understand,
>> and you shall indeed see but never perceive.
> For this people's heart has grown dull,
>> and their ears are heavy of hearing,
>> and their eyes they have closed,
> lest they should perceive with their eyes,
>> and hear with their ears,
> and understand with their heart,
>> and turn for me to heal them.'"

In John's Gospel we read that Jesus analyzed this attitude more fully. "How can you believe, who receive glory from one another and do not seek the glory that comes from the only God?" (John 5:44): you are too anxious to please and be approved by one's fel-

lows, one's class, one's circle to see clearly where truth and good-
ness lie. "You do not believe, because you do not belong to my
sheep" (John 10:26): you are not spiritually ready to follow me.
"If you continue in my word . . . you will know the truth." John
himself explains: "This is the judgment, that the light has come
into the world, and men loved darkness rather than light, because their deeds were evil. For every one who does evil hates the
light. . . . But he who does what is true comes to the light" (John
3:19ff.).

5. It is because his appeal is to reason, common sense, experience,
   conscience, "the inner light" that Jesus frequently expresses surprise that people do not see for themselves the truth of what he
   says and does: "How is it you fail to perceive? . . . Do you not
   see?" . . . "Are you also still without understanding?" Good fathers are careful what they give to children; faithful shepherds
   search anxiously for lost sheep; loving parents watch longingly
   for the return of wayward sons; is it not *obvious* that God does so
   too — and more so?

Such then is the important assessment of the nature and need of humanity that lies behind such expressions as "right judgment," "ability
to interpret," and "the light within you"; Jesus believed in the individual's capacity to recognize truth when presented with it and when
given the will to do so. His persistent questioning was aimed at awak-
ening that capacity. It is nowhere suggested that the rational and sincere man's "light" is sufficient of itself to live by, or to find God by. He
needs Christ. But when he is presented with divine truth and is willing
to accept it and explore it, the truth will justify itself to him.

This is the answer to any question about Christ's "authority."
That men felt his authority as they listened and watched is abundantly
clear. The common people exclaimed at it; leading people challenged
it; a military commander respected it; temple officials acknowledged
it; unclean spirits, wind and wave "obeyed" it. When questioned about
his authority, Jesus asked his critics what they thought of the Baptist's

authority: was it divine, or just human? They refused to answer, saying they did not know, for they feared the reaction whatever they said. So Jesus refused to reply: if they did not know authority when confronted with it, the question was idle. Authority must shine by its own light, be seen, felt, discerned: if that was not admitted when seen, there was no value in arguing about it.

Jesus never demanded blind obedience, as though claiming "I am the Son of God, you must listen to me." He sought the assent of the unbiased mind and the clear conscience observing the truth of what he said and the moral quality of what he did. Sometimes, as at Nazareth, he would remind hearers of the Scriptures on which their judgment had been nourished, showing (often to their surprise) how his life and words coincided with revered teaching. At other times he insisted not on the miraculous nature of his deeds but on their value. Challenged with unlawfully healing on the Sabbath, his defense was that he was doing *good* on the Sabbath, undoing Satan's bonds upon a woman, healing the paralyzed, liberating the possessed, delivering, enlightening, restoring sanity. "I have shown you many good works from the Father: for which of these do you stone me?" "Believe me for the very works' sake. . . . The works which the Father has granted me to accomplish, these very works which I am doing, bear me witness that the Father has sent me."

This appeal to reason and value, to mind and conscience, is in the last resort the surest foundation of truth. In fact, there is no other, not the visible trappings of authority, the exaltation of office, the assumption of superiority, the threat of punishment for denial. Reason and value, self-evident to the honest mind and the clear conscience — these are the hallmarks of authority. There are no others. The questioning Christ stands ever among us, seeking our assent.

7

Jesus the Realist

THE MOST PERSISTENT, and most misleading, caricature of Jesus assumes without the slightest foundation that he was always tolerant, lenient, peaceable, never angry, never even forceful in attitude or speech. The fanciful line in a children's hymn, "Gentle Jesus, meek and mild," seriously distorts the whole divine portrait, making the master appear helpless and futile in the face of the enormous problems of violence and evil in modern society — a sentimentalist on a battlefield. That image is nonsense.

No one can deny the immediate sympathy and exquisite insight Jesus revealed when the occasion called for it. But to see nothing else in Jesus is to be blind to his moral strength, his clear-eyed candor, his sometimes frightening indignation. We read that the disciples were "afraid" to ask Jesus about his death, to tell what they had been discussing, to intrude upon his preoccupied mood. Priests and scribes are said to have feared him, and once "no one dared ask him any question."

Who would have wanted to crucify a harmless, unarmed, passivist village carpenter with innocent romantic views on life, people, and society? A coalition of a Roman procurator, a regional "king," present and former high priests, the Jewish Sanhedrin, and the Jerusalem crowd thought it necessary to silence and remove him by violence. That is the measure of Jesus' forthrightness, realism, authority, and threat to the existing state of things.

One may sense something of this realism in Jesus' reaction to flattery. He hated insincerity. "Why do you call me good?" he demands of one who apparently is being superficially polite in posing a question. And when Nicodemus, "a teacher of Israel," begins a conversation with an elaborate introduction: "Rabbi, we know that you are a teacher come from God; for no one can do these signs that you do, unless God is with him . . . ," Jesus breaks in to bring him at once to the point — the issue between self-salvation by the law and salvation by divine regeneration. "Truly, truly, I say to you, unless one is born anew, he cannot see the kingdom of God." Seeking a charge against him, spies prepared a trap question, beginning "Teacher, we know that you speak and teach rightly, and show no partiality, but truly teach the way of God. Is it lawful for us to give tribute to Caesar?" Ignoring the praise Jesus poses immediately the crucial question: whose coinage were they using? That answered their question. Mere wordplay got nowhere with Jesus.

Contrary to popular assumptions, Jesus did *not* "see only the best in all men." Certainly he saw what men might become if they accepted the grace of God; but he "needed no one to bear witness of man; for he himself knew what was in man" and he "did not trust himself to them" (John 2:24). He listed, relentlessly, the evils within that came "out of the heart of man, . . . evil thoughts, fornication, theft, murder, adultery, coveting, wickedness, deceit, licentiousness, envy, slander, pride, foolishness." Nothing sentimental about that analysis of human conduct!

So he could describe in his parables a whole rogue's gallery of examples. From Luke alone we can gather: the professional prostitute, whose sins were many; the shallow triflers with religious issues who sounded like children playing; the heartless priest, unconscious of social duty; the indifferent Levite, ignoring the needy; the churlish neighbor, impatient of a simple request; the hypocritical Pharisees, hiding truth from the common people; the blasphemer against light, therefore beyond forgiveness; the moneymaking farmer with no thought beyond his barns; the callous legalists, ranking regulations above human suffering; the crafty king, ruling by foxlike cunning; the trivial-minded, offering childish excuses; the ungrateful youth rebelling against restraint; the dishonest steward, embezzling his master's capital; the unfeeling glutton, ignoring the beggar at his door; the corrupter of the vulnerable, better never born; the slave-driving boss, demanding supper at once; the unjust judge, needing to be "plagued" into doing his duty; the self-righteous bigot, parading his piety; the lazy servant, hoarding money entrusted for use; the flattery-loving scribe, delighting in obsequious tributes; the ruthless moneylender, mortgaging a widow's home; the faithless servants carousing in their lord's absence; the treacherous disciple, betraying his master; the tyrant rulers, calling themselves "Benefactors"; the unreliable friend, boasting loyalty yet denying; religious lawyers who made religion burdensome for others; the elder brother, lacking forgiveness and affection; public opponents asking "loaded" questions ("he perceived their craftiness"); hair-splitting "theologians" who "have a fine way of rejecting God's commands" by citing mere traditions.

How can it ever have been thought that Jesus saw people through rose-tinted spectacles?

Since he moved open-eyed among such people, it is no wonder that Jesus' speech is often sharp. He preaches the value of life under God's reign, but it is the quislings who work for Rome and the harlots who enter the kingdom before Jewry's religious leaders. His irony is abrasive: an embezzling steward teaches "wisdom" to the pious; Peter's "What shall we have?" evokes the promise of "a throne, each, and a judge's robes!" Had the crowds expected to find the Baptist (of all people!) a waving reed, or a silk-clad dandy? No prophet entirely lacks followers — except at home. But it would never do for a prophet to perish outside Jerusalem. At one point the disciples tell Jesus that the Pharisees were offended at his speech, almost suggesting that he moderate his language.

Jesus' actions could be equally stern. There is nothing sentimental about his outburst at the priests' exploitation of their monopoly in
sacrifices and currency exchange. Nor in his attitude to Herod, whose
vicious silencing of the Baptist earned him the terrible silence of Jesus.
He warned intending disciples to expect homelessness; to be ready for
conflict, bringing scrip and sword; and to bring their own crosses with
them. They go as sheep among wolves. Temptations will certainly
come; he knows the moral climate of that Roman world. The love of
many will grow cold.

To the disciples themselves Jesus is no less forthright. "Behind
me, Satan!" was addressed to Peter when he briefly spoke as the "adver-
sary" (Hebrew "satan") of Jesus. Later, Jesus asks Peter, "Do you love
me?" three times to retract his threefold denial of Christ — as Peter
grievingly perceives. Jesus' forgiveness was no easy "let-off." "Could
you not watch *one hour?*" Jesus asks in Gethsemane of men who had
promised loyalty *"unto death."* When James and John, incensed at the
refusal of Samaritans to give Jesus hospitality, suggested he should call
down fire upon them, Jesus rebuked his men and led them away; some
ancient copies of Luke spell out the rebuke as "you do not know what
manner of spirit you are of." And when many turned back from following him, Jesus asked the Twelve, "Will you also go away?" challenging them to reaffirm their loyalty. Some imitators — miracle
mongers, exorcists, "prophets" using his name — will face firm rejection in the end: "Depart from me, I never knew you." Jesus uses other
expressions to describe final judgment that are equally brusque: "the
door is shut"; "outer darkness"; and "eternal punishment" are as typi-
cally Christ's as his "Come to me, all you who labor. . . ."

Jesus states unwelcome facts with similar bluntness. The storm
will beat on the house of the obedient man as fiercely as on that of the
disobedient; God sends his rain on the just and the unjust. The rich
have special difficulty in entering God's kingdom, and some men have
not the gift of self-restraint (Matt. 19:11ff.). The eager young appli-
cant for discipleship must sell, give, and come — or be allowed to go
his way. The result of Jesus' ministry is not always peace. With unsen-

timental realism he describes his own mission as fire-raising, sword brandishing, and as dividing families. Similarly he describes without softening, and in detail, the death that awaits himself. Some who stray may be sought and carried home, but the willful selfish younger son must taste loneliness and hunger, a long trudge alone from the far country, and the humiliation of begging a place among his father's servants. Though Jesus defends the woman "taken in adultery" from her hypocritical accusers and declines himself to condemn her, yet his last words to her are uncompromising: "Go, and sin no more."

It is scarcely too much to say that Jesus' tongue had its decidedly rough edge, and he could be deliberately provocative. When he praised a Roman's faith he contrasted it with the unbelief he met in Judah. To highlight Jewry's impenitence he cited the penitence of heathen Tyre, Sidon, and Sodom. To illustrate love of neighbor he chose a good Samaritan (a despised foreigner), just as he emphasized the gratitude of one out of ten healed lepers by citing him as "this foreigner." He compared Jewish leaders in their pious array to the wayside sepulchres whitened every festival time to prevent pilgrims incurring accidental "uncleanness." He has a very sharp word for Pharisees who use cosmetics to emphasize the rigor of their fasting (Matt. 6:16) and for those who "sound a trumpet" to draw attention to their gifts at synagogue. (It is said that such treasury chests were trumpet-shaped, and a coin deftly spun would roll round and round.)

In the heat of controversy, phrases like "brood of vipers," "that fox" Herod, "blind fools," hypocrites, "perverse generation," "how long am I to bear with you?" fell from Christ's lips. As we shall see, he was skilled in controversial questioning, and especially provoking was his readiness to attack his opponents on what they considered their greatest virtue, their understanding and defense of scripture. Jesus showed none of the "religious sentiment" that avoids all controversy, lets things pass, and keeps the peace at the expense of truth, sincerity, and loyalty to God.

All in all, it is not surprising that when Jesus asked his disciples who men were saying that he was, they could report that, though some suggested he was the sad and gentle Jeremiah, others found it possible to suppose he was Elijah — Elijah of the wild appearance, the harsh threats, the fierce opposition to Israel's "halting between two opinions," and the calling down of fire.

Of course this is just one side of the "total Christ." But it is not untruthful. And it is a necessary corrective to much popular misrepresentation of Jesus as a romantic idealist who would not oppose or condemn anything, nor ever speak sharply, even to the devil. That false picture has produced nurseries of gentle Christians, meek and mild in the face of appalling evils, and a church too often capable of being ignored.

8

Jesus on the Old Testament

T HAT JESUS KNEW thoroughly, and reverenced, the Old Testament
is beyond question; his recorded sayings include fifty-one quotations from it and some fifty-four echoes of its words. Copies of the
scriptures being scarce and expensive, others asked, "Whence has this
man this learning?" The answer was that his acquaintance came from
attentive and retentive listening at synagogue. Much of his public
teaching was commentary on Old Testament themes, and among
them he found his messianic mission and persona, the Servant-Mes-
siah. He had an unfaltering sense of continuity with God's past revelation and declared "scripture cannot be broken." From the Old Testament he explained his death to bewildered disciples — "what is
written about me has its fulfillment" — and he died with its words on
his lips.

Yet Jesus was never a rabbi, a scribe, or the head of a synagogue,
and his use of the Old Testament deeply offended the orthodox. The
reasons are not difficult to discover.

Jesus held that Old Testament principles were often good but inadequate. In his "sermon on the mount" he repeats several times, "You
have heard that it was said . . . ," citing some accepted rule, adding,
"But I say to you. . . ." He insists that he did not come to destroy the

46

law, not the least stroke of the pen, or to lower the Old Testament standards, but to "fulfill," to extend and internalize, its precepts. The law condemns murder; in God's kingdom anger, insult, and contempt are equally condemned. The law condemns adultery; in God's kingdom lust also is condemned. The Old Testament forbids false oaths "by God . . ."; in God's kingdom swearing "by heaven," "by earth," or "by my head" is also forbidden. The Old Testament limits retaliation to only an eye for an eye; in God's kingdom injury is to be accepted without revenge. Love toward a fellow Jew (as the Old Testament was then understood) must in God's kingdom be extended to any neighbor, enemy, or persecutor, as God's love is.

So Jesus upholds and yet criticizes the Old Testament standards as external, concerned with conduct but neglecting underlying character; as inclined to punish rather than to cure; and as confined to Jews. As Jesus says, the righteousness of the people of the kingdom must *exceed* that of the scribes. His "I say to you . . ." has a most regal sound.

In Jesus' eyes, therefore, the Old Testament is insufficient, and in consequence temporary. One inquirer, having fulfilled the commandments, still sought eternal life; he was told that he must *also* sell all and follow Jesus. The law and the prophets, Jesus declares, were valid only "until John" — since then, the kingdom is preached. "Blessed are your eyes . . . [and] your ears, . . ." said Jesus to the Twelve, for you see and hear what many prophets longed to, but did not.

Jesus' disciples did not keep the customary fasts as other Jews were doing because *they* had the Bridegroom with them, and sadness was out of place. The new gospel of the kingdom would destroy the old wineskins of Judaism. The new cloth of the fresh revelation could not be used to patch the tattered garments of Judaism — a trenchant and far-reaching judgment. Those who busily search the Old Testament seeking eternal life still must come to Jesus (of whom the Old Testament tells) to find it (John 5:39ff.). In all these ways Jesus is insisting that the Old Testament is preparatory, needing fulfillment to become effective. In Jewish ears, such a view would sound blasphemous.

But that was not all: Jesus handled the Old Testament with a sovereign freedom of interpretation and sublime authority, sometimes infuriating his hearers. Elijah's foreign succor at Zarephath and Elisha's dealing with the foreign commander Naaman, both demonstrating that prophets were often more honored abroad than at home, were cited to explain his own rejection at Nazareth. Malachi's promise that Elijah would return was fulfilled in the appearing of Jesus' forerunner, John. Moses' accolade for outstanding godliness — "names written in heaven" — Jesus applied to his own disciples. Moses' celebrated manna was said by Jesus not to be the true bread from heaven; that was he who came down from heaven to give his flesh for the life of the world.

Moses' brazen serpent prefigured Christ's cross; Sodom and Gomorrah were warnings to Christ's generation of the peril of rejecting God's word; Jonah's conversion of pagan Nineveh and the queen of Sheba's visit to Solomon are rebukes to Christ's unrepentant hearers. Jesus is the true living water foreshadowed in the water from the rock, celebrated at the Feast of Tabernacles. He is the good shepherd promised by Ezekiel, the stone (of Psalm 118) rejected by so-called expert builders but ordained to become head of the corner in God's building.

Jesus prophesied the destruction of the Temple, despite the Old Testament's assumption of divine protection, and applied Jeremiah's words about a den of thieves to the current Temple market in sacrifices and currency. He gathered the blind and lame into the Temple court, against the law, and used Hosea's words "I desire mercy and not sacrifice" to exalt the importance of kindness above all ritual. Isaiah's warning about seeing without perceiving and hearing without understanding becomes Jesus' explanation of people's puzzlement over his parables. And he quotes Isaiah's exuberant words about the Spirit's being upon him to declare the blessings of return from exile and rebuilding the waste cities (Isa. 61:1ff.) as fulfilled by his own preaching of God's kingdom in the synagogue at Nazareth.

In part, this use of Old Testament language to express very new ideas was but a teaching aid: the sacred language and well-known texts would resonate in the hearers' minds and carry a weight that new terms would lack. It was the usual method of the scribes to find justification for their teaching in very odd, sometimes unmeaning and even misspelled phrases of scripture. But the Jewish authorities knew that in the ears of Jesus' hearers the use of such language gave Old Testament authority to new things — and they were incensed. It is significant, for all that, that Jesus never pressed an Old Testament statement to "squeeze" out of it some remote implication far from the writer's intention, as Matthew (for example) does with the word "Nazarene" (Matt. 2:23), and Paul does with the word "seed" (Gal. 3:16 Greek, and so KJV).

But Jesus' very free interpretation of ancient scripture went further. The ambiguous words of Psalm 82 — "You are gods" — he uses to defend his claim to divine sonship. Another psalmist's reference to the perfect praise of babes is cited to justify the excitement of children on Palm Sunday as he came to the city. Zechariah's prophecy about Messiah on a donkey he deliberately fulfills by his entry to Jerusalem — a kind of enacted blasphemy in Jewish eyes. Isaiah's parable about God's fruitless vineyard is made to foretell the killing of prophets — his own death — and the giving of God's vineyard, Israel, to other tenants: non-Jews. Indeed, privately, Jesus says that he and his followers are the true vine of God henceforth.

By defining the greatest commandment as love of God and neighbor and adding "on these two commandments depend all the law and the prophets," Jesus in effect disposes of the whole Old Testament except for two verses, or so his enemies could claim. Similarly, Jesus radically reinterpreted the entire Old Testament promise of messianic deliverance, retaining "kingdom" language but defining "kingdom" not in terms of political freedom and sovereignty, but in terms of social good for the blind, lame, poor, prisoners, and others. In the same way, Jesus openly challenged current expectation of a messianic "Son of David", a title implying both descent from and similarity to the hero king David, dismissing it as nonsense: if the Messiah is the son of David, how could David call him "Lord" (Ps. 110:1)?

Jesus insisted that the kingdom promised was the inward rule of God within the heart, and when Peter said "Thou art the Christ," Jesus immediately began to speak of his death. Yet all this was "as it is written," though no one else had read it so. Consonant with this is his transformation of the most sacred Passover feast into the Lord's Supper, and Abraham's (and Jeremiah's) promise of a covenant between Israel and God into a pledge of salvation through his own blood.

This wholesale retranslation of seminal Old Testament ideas was accompanied by his de-emphasis of circumcision, animal sacrifice, Israel's unique election as God's people (a centurion and a Syrophoenician earn commendation for great faith, and the gospel is to be sent to all nations), Sabbath-keeping, "uncleanness" rules, and tithing as having little relative significance in God's kingdom. In this royal liberty of interpretation lies the meaning of the later title, "Lord of Scripture."

Yet Jesus does more still.

Jesus showed the Old Testament to be at several points self-contradictory. Already in his temptation Jesus answered the devil's scripture with contrary scripture. To the scribes' insistence that oaths *must* be performed, even when in temper a son dedicates everything to God, Jesus countered with the law that required sons to honor (and maintain) their parents. Challenged because his disciples plucked corn on the Sabbath, Jesus cited David's taking the legally forbidden showbread in the shrine for his hungry men. Another time, Jesus cited the law requiring priests to work on the Sabbath, and another requiring circumcision to be performed on the Sabbath. Criticized for healing on the Sabbath, Jesus demanded whether it was lawful to do good on the Sabbath, or to undo Satan's work. Thereby Jesus appealed to the Old Testament's concern for compassion and at the same time extended the argument to animals and their owners' duty to feed or to rescue them from harm even on the Sabbath. Questioned about divorce, Jesus opposed to Moses' "concessionary" right of divorce the original purpose of God in Genesis, that man and wife should become indissolubly one. In each of these instances, Jesus was offering a *moral* criticism of legalism, making a moral decision on which scripture to obey, and setting conscience above documents. No scribe could condone that kind of distinction.

Finally, in his own behavior and attitudes Jesus ignored or rejected some of the precedents and assumptions assumed to possess Old Testament authority. He did not, for example, observe the frequent ritual washing of hands that orthodox Jews expected. Asked to comment on the birth of a blind child, which the rabbis debated as proving the sinfulness either of the parent or of the unborn infant, Jesus refused both "explanations," insisting that what mattered was to heal the blindness. Similarly, when he was invited to draw the usual conclusion about certain people killed by a falling tower or others brutally executed by Pilate, Jesus denied that such victims of accident or violence were necessarily greater sinners than others — all must be prepared for tragedy, by living in penitence. Rules about ritual uncleanness (of lepers and others) Jesus ignored.

Challenged about his claim to forgive sins (in the Old Testament, by implication, the prerogative of God alone), Jesus demonstrated his authority by healing the paralyzed man. Since in Jewish thought the cause of suffering (sin) must be removed before healing was possible, Jesus' healing the man implied his ability to forgive the man's sins as well. Confronted with an adulteress and asked to confirm Moses' sentence of stoning, Jesus simply refused. Facing the refusal of certain Samaritans to entertain him and advised to call down fire upon them, as Elijah did upon his opponents, Jesus again refused and rebuked the suggestion (some ancient copies of Luke do not mention Elijah, but the precedent was implied nevertheless). In neither of these instances did Jesus accept the Old Testament rule, or assumption, or example, as a word of God for himself. He judged by his own conscience what was of permanent authority and what was better ignored.

It is plainly not true that (as is sometimes suggested) Jesus accepted the Old Testament as divinely inspired "from cover to cover for all time." To listen to him carefully, and watch him closely, is to realize how cautious, how discriminating, his study of the scriptures was, alongside his delight, his appreciation, and his appeal to many parts of the sacred book of his people. Our Lord Jesus is, very clearly, the Lord of Scripture.

9

Jesus on Salvation: Conduct, Character, Belief

THE INITIAL CALL of Jesus to his first disciples was not to listen, to learn, or to believe, but to "follow" him — an invitation to adventure, to share experience, to imitate an example. According to the tradition of his ministry preserved in the first three Gospels, this emphasis upon practical readjustment in behavior, upon right and good living, remained absolutely paramount in all Christ's teaching.

In Matthew's "sermon on the mount," Jesus refers to matters of character, the sort of person one is, some twenty-four times (the figure is swollen by seven "beatitudes"); he refers to conduct, the sort of things one does, some thirty-nine times. Perhaps the sharpest sentence in the whole sermon is, "For I tell you, unless your righteousness exceeds that of the scribes and Pharisees, you will never enter the kingdom of heaven." Consonant with this is the warning: "Whoever relaxes one of the least of these commandments, and teaches men so, shall be called least in the kingdom of heaven. . . . He who does them and teaches them shall be called great." And Jesus proceeds to extend and deepen the interpretation of several "commandments."

This reinforcement of the essentially practical demands of Jewish religion is repeated again and again:

> "Whatever you wish that men would do to you, do so to them, *for this is the law and the prophets.*"
>
> "You shall love the Lord your God with all your heart, and with all your soul, and with all your mind. . . . You shall love your neighbor as yourself. *On these two commandments depend all the law and the prophets.*"
>
> "Is it lawful on the Sabbath to do good or to do harm?"

In a phrase, the essence of Judaism is, after all, good conduct. And that is likewise essential to life in Christ's kingdom:

> "Not every one who says to me, 'Lord, Lord,' shall enter the kingdom of heaven, but he who *does the will* of my Father who is in heaven."
>
> "Many will claim to have prophesied, . . . cast out demons, . . . done many mighty works" all in Christ's name, only to be rejected as unknown by him because of their evil conduct.

But neither profession, nor performance, nor proximity to Christ avails without obedience. And Jesus continues:

> "Every tree that does not bear good fruit is cut down and thrown into the fire. Thus you will know them by their fruits."
>
> "Every one who hears these words of mine *and does them* will be like a wise man who built his house upon the rock. . . . every one who hears these words of mine and *does not do them* will be like a foolish man who built his house upon the sand. . . ."
>
> Merely *knowing* what is good and right and true does not save one's house of life when the storm breaks, but only *doing* as such knowledge directs.

"Whoever *does* the will of my Father in heaven is my brother, and sister, and mother."

"A man had two sons; and he went to the first and said, 'Son, go and work in the vineyard.' . . . He answered, 'I will not'; but afterward he repented and went. And he went to the second son and said the same; and he answered, 'I go, sir,' but did not go. Which of the two did the will of his father?" — a stern warning about the unimportance of religious profession alone.

"When the Son of man comes in his glory . . . he will sit on his glorious throne. Before him will be gathered all the nations, and he will separate them . . . as a shepherd separates the sheep from the goats. . . . Then the King will say to those at his right hand, 'Come, O blessed of my Father, inherit the kingdom prepared for you . . . ; for I was hungry, . . . thirsty, . . . a stranger, . . . naked, . . . sick, . . . in prison and you came to me.' Then the righteous will answer him, 'Lord, when did we . . . ?' And the King will answer, . . . 'As you did it to one of the least of these my brethren, you did it to me.' Then he will say to those on his left hand, 'Depart from me, you cursed. . . . As you did it not to one of the least of these, you did it not to me.'"

In the last resort, Jesus says plainly, deeds determine destiny. And the emphasis upon conduct continues to the very last verses of Matthew's Gospel, where Jesus commissions his disciples — and the future church — to "'Go . . . and make disciples, . . . teaching them to observe all that I have commanded you. . . .'" In Matthew's eyes, nothing could be clearer, more central, or more urgent than to *do* the will of God as Jesus has expounded it.

Luke echoes Matthew's emphasis at several points, and adds a few other examples. When a lawyer asks the secret of eternal life, Jesus inquires how he understood the law. The lawyer cited the commandments to love God and one's neighbor, to which Jesus replied, "You have answered right; *do this,* and you will live." The lawyer then asks,

"Who is my neighbor?" to which Jesus answers with the parable of the good Samaritan and the question, "Which of these three" (priest, levite, Samaritan) "proved neighbor to the man who fell among robbers?" The lawyer said, "The one who showed mercy on him." And yet again Jesus underlined the crucial point: "Go, and *do* likewise." Mark's version has the suggestion that to know the truth about this question is to be "not far" from the kingdom, but not yet in it; that involves acting upon what one knows. John has a similar utterance: "If you know these things, blessed are you if you do them."

Whatever needs to be added to supplement or analyze this emphasis of Jesus upon conduct, nothing — absolutely *nothing* — must be allowed to obscure it or to take its place. To allow that would be, not misunderstanding, but disobedience.

Yet this emphasis upon visible conduct does have one danger that Jewish legalism did not escape, that of externalism and hypocrisy, doing what will be approved simply to be seen of men. Jesus insists that outward behavior must be genuine in motive and purpose. Almsgiving, for example, so emphasized in Judaism, must not be advertised with a view to public praise, but must be genuinely generous and *secret;* prayer, too, must not be paraded "on the corners of the streets" but kept private and simple; fasting (also required in Judaism) must never be performed as religious display but as private self-discipline. Jesus stresses that in all such matters we are dealing with the Father who "sees in secret" the inner motives of every soul, the character behind the conduct.

Luke tells of Jesus' confrontation with Zacchaeus, a reputed sinner (because though a Jew he operated the Roman tax laws within Jewry, much to his own profit). When Jesus noticed and spoke to him, Zacchaeus responded "joyfully," and when Jesus was criticized for his action, Zacchaeus vowed to give away half his fortune and to restore fourfold anything he had taken by fraud. Jesus replies, very significantly, "Today salvation has come to this house, . . . For the Son of man came to seek and to save the lost." Clearly, it was not the redistribution of wealth that prompted Jesus' warm words, but the undoing of wrong and the total change in the man himself, his motives, attitude to the needy, and the social responsibility involved in his career. Such transformation of personality, manifest in conduct, is "salvation." Jesus says so.

The relation of inward character to outward behavior is one of Jesus' frequent themes. The "beatitudes" which open Matthew's "sermon on the mount" describe a type of person who is deliberately contrasted with the type that human society normally produces, admires, and so often rewards. Poverty, meekness, purity of heart, peaceableness, and willingness to suffer persecution are not qualities that make for worldly success, but they alone delineate the type of character that will produce the behavior Jesus requires. Accused of doing good by Satan's help, Jesus demands, "Either make the tree good and its fruit good, or make the tree bad and its fruit bad. For the tree is known by its fruit. . . . How can you speak good when you are evil? For out of the overflow of the heart the mouth speaks" (NIV). Jesus adds, "The good man out of his treasure brings forth good, and the evil man out of his evil treasure brings forth evil." The principle that moral well-doing can be expected only from moral well-being could hardly be more clearly stated.

Jesus again uses the analogy of tree and fruit when speaking of false prophets: "You will know them by their fruits. Are grapes gathered from thorns, or figs from thistles?" The inner nature governs the outer product. But he also suggests that such false prophets "come to you in sheep's clothing but inwardly are ravening wolves." Again, he likens hypocrites to tombs "outwardly . . . beautiful, but within full of dead men's bones and all uncleanness," whitewashed at festival times to prevent pilgrims accidentally contracting ritual uncleanness. "So you also outwardly appear righteous to men, but within you are full of hypocrisy and iniquity." And he pursues the contrast between inner character and outward behavior by describing those who diligently cleanse the outside of cups and plates while neglecting the inside, which is "full of extortion and rapacity."

Replying to debate about "unclean" (defiling) meats, Jesus

roundly declared that nothing going into a man defiles him, but "from within, out of the heart of man, come evil thoughts, fornication, theft, murder, adultery, coveting, wickedness, deceit, licentiousness, an evil eye, slander, pride, foolishness. All these evil things come from within, and they defile a man."

So in the teaching of Jesus, conduct is of supreme importance, but conduct cannot be considered apart from the character from which it issues. The significance of this insight is clear in the constant references in apostolic preaching and writing to the necessity of repentance, conversion, regeneration, new birth, "a new creature," "the new man in Christ," the old self "crucified with Christ" and "risen with him to newness of life." The new standard of conduct required by Jesus cannot be reached by unaided human nature: the whole inner self must be transformed in attitude and resources if the outward behavior, speech, relationships, and dedication to worthwhile ends that Jesus calls for are to be achieved. So the gospel which offers inward renewal becomes indeed "good news" to sinful men and women, making the Christian ideal practical.

In the earlier Gospels, this spiritual and psychological change whose value will be proved by the conduct it produces is to be achieved by "following" Jesus, watching, hearing, sharing in his company. *Listening* to his conversation, his questions, his answers to others' questions, and his prayers was a central element in that experience, and surprising importance is attached to it. "Take heed then how you hear," Jesus warns, for careless hearing, without understanding or obeying, incurs judgment. "He who rejects me and does not receive my sayings has a judge; the word that I have spoken will be his judge on the last day" (John 12:47-48).

The importance of hearing and "keeping" Christ's sayings is underlined thirty-five times in the Gospels. Hearing his word is having seed sown in one's heart (six references); at the Transfiguration, God himself says, "Listen to him"; Jesus, too, calls people to "hear, and understand." It is repeatedly affirmed that "many pressed to hear Jesus," including tax collectors and worshipers in the Temple, and they "hung upon his words." In previous generations, Jesus said, "many had longed to hear" what his generation were hearing. Those who do hear and keep his words are his close family, mother, sisters, brothers. When one woman declared his mother blessed in such a son, he replied, "Blessed are they that hear the word of God and keep it." His sheep hear his voice, recognize and follow him, and are safe. Luke notes Mary sitting at Jesus' feet, "listening"; the disciples generally are described as "you that hear"; and in his great Upper Room prayer, Jesus can say, "I have given them the words which thou gavest me . . . and they have kept thy word."

Already the teaching of Jesus sorts men out: "every one that is of the truth hears my voice"; "Why do you not understand what I say? It is because you cannot bear to hear my word. . . . He who is of God hears the words of God; the reason why you do not hear them is that you are not of God." To his missioners Jesus says, "If any one will not listen to your words, shake off the dust from your feet as you leave. . . . It shall be more tolerable in the day of judgment for . . . Sodom and Gomorrah than for that town." And again, "he who hears you hears me: he who rejects you rejects me . . . and him who sent me." On the other hand, Jesus affirms most definitely, "Truly, truly, I say to you, he who hears my word and believes him who sent me, has eternal life."

That conjunction of "hearing" with "believing" is significant. For, of course, this hearing and listening to Jesus of which the earlier Gospels are so full were not possible after Christ's ascension. From then onward, throughout history, "hearing Jesus" has been replaced by "believing" the testimony that the eyewitnesses bore to him. So Paul replies to "What must I do to be saved?" with the direct instruction, "Believe in the Lord Jesus and you will be saved." He later explains "the word of faith which we preach" by saying, "if you confess with your lips that Jesus is Lord, and believe in your heart that God raised him from the dead, you will be saved."

In the sixty-eight chapters of Matthew, Mark, and Luke, "belief" is mentioned forty-three times; in John's twenty-one chapters it is mentioned ninety-one times. It is this faith in Christ, in his words, his works, his saving death, his being sent by God, his power to save, that in apostolic thought is the only hope for the sinful to become a new self, thus making possible the new Christlike character from which issues Christlike behavior.

Unfortunately, this form of expression led in some quarters to an inversion of emphasis. Belief, or faith, became the prior demand; the good conduct that Jesus insisted upon became at best the hoped-for consequence, but often the merely assumed consequence, of such faith. Christians were no longer "disciples" but "believers," and the expected moral change had repeatedly to be urged, and its absence deplored. Thus we find the epistle of James arguing strongly that faith without works is "dead"; 2 Peter exhorting readers to add to their faith moral excellence, knowledge, self-control, steadfastness, godliness, brotherly affection, and love; and 1 John reciting thirteen reasons why the true Christian may not sin (3:3-10; compare 2:3-11). "Belief" had too often come to mean merely religious opinion, a set of ideas that needed to be translated into character and conduct by "every effort" of will, instead of a living relationship with Christ that transformed the self into his image and one's whole life into his likeness.

This shift of emphasis produced the strong contention that arose in the first four centuries about orthodoxy — the right interpretation of theological ideas — and in time the dreadful persecution of "heretics" or even of dissidents who dared to question, or simply to explore, the "received" version of Christian doctrine. In such ways the demand for Christ's pattern of conduct, the whole thrust of Christ's own teaching, was overlaid by an emphasis upon intellectual conformity that ended in most un-Christlike behavior.

The essential truth is that an overmastering conviction that Jesus is the Son of God, the Lord and Savior and the ideal of human excellence, does transform the self. And that transformation, unhindered by doubts or looking backward, will by God's help produce the sort of conduct upon which Jesus placed such emphasis. That is salvation.

IO

Jesus' Idea of the Church

THE OLD ENGLISH WORD "church" occurs among the sayings of Jesus only twice (Matt. 16:18, 18:17), where it translates the Greek word "ecclesia," meaning a group or assembly "called out" for some corporate purpose. The "town's regular assembly" at Ephesus was called an "ecclesia" (Acts 19:39), and for Jews it was already familiar from the Greek Old Testament for the people of God "called out" of heathenism to be his possession and agents in the earth. At the time Matthew wrote it was an appropriate term to apply to the Christian movement.

At first, Christians were "the people of the Way," another "sect" of Judaism along side the Pharisees, Sadducees, and Essenes (Acts 9:2, 24:14), meeting in private houses or hired halls (Acts 2:46, 12:12, Rom. 16:5, 1 Cor. 16:19, Philem. 2, Acts 19:9); "church" never means a building in the New Testament. Jesus had warned that the vineyard of God would be passed to new tenants, that he and his men were the "true vine" of God's planting, and the church soon knew herself to be that new "called out people," the new Israel of faith (Rom. 2:28ff., 4:4-17, chaps. 9-11).

Clearly, Jesus contemplated the continuance of his ministry through the group he had gathered and those who were to believe in him through their word (John 17:20), bound together by loyalty to himself. Yet he left them hardly more than memories of life in his company, a few instructions, a rudimentary leadership, a charge to love one another, and two or three immense promises. He provided no material resources and only the very minimum of organization: a significant way in which to welcome new disciples, and a simple ceremony of remembrance and dedication when disciples shared meals.

When Peter declared, "You are the Christ, the Son of the living God," Jesus replied, "Blessed are you, Simon Bar-Jona! For flesh and blood has not revealed this to you, but my Father who is in heaven. And I tell you, you are Peter [a rock], and on this rock I will build my church." Thus, the individual confessing the messiahship and divine sonship of Jesus is to be the foundation stone of the coming church — not the individual Galilean named Simon, himself, alone, nor the abstract virtue, faith, but every individual who stands where Peter stood, who knows the Father's revelation which Peter knew, and confesses what Peter confessed. The sum of such individuals in each place, each generation, and all together form the "called out" people of God. They will be henceforth "the body of Christ," to inherit the memories of Jesus and witness of him to the world. As in their earlier missions, this proselytizing testimony was to be in compassionate service to all manner of human needs (see Matt. 10:7ff.), not in preaching only.

The precise instruction ran: "Go . . . and make disciples of all nations, baptizing them in the name of the Father and of the Son and of the Holy Spirit, teaching them to observe all that I have commanded you." This commission, looking beyond Israel, concentrating upon discipleship and obedience, and marking the adherence of new disciples by baptism into the protection, possession, and control of God, defines the task, the range, and the method of growth of the church for all time — and excludes all other ambitions.

The use of the threefold divine name in baptism in Matthew 28:19 *may* owe something to later development in the Gentile world when it became necessary to make clear which of many gods was invoked. Baptism originated in the Jewish washing of proselytes from

paganism entering the chosen people (note Acts 22:16); it was modi-
fied by John the Baptist's application of it to Jews themselves in repentant self-cleansing as preparation for Messiah; and it was enriched by
the example and experience of Jesus, whose baptism was accompanied
by assurance of his divine sonship, God's pleasure in him, and the en-
dowment with the Holy Spirit for his work. John 4:1-3 suggests that
Jesus did at least approve, if not conduct, such baptism during his
ministry. The "washing" implication was later supplemented (especially by Paul) with the implication of death and burial with Christ
and resurrection to new life (Rom. 6). The baptismal confession seems
to have become simply "Jesus is Lord" (Rom. 10:9, Acts 16:31, Phil.
2:11).

A second instruction established a pattern of remembrance and
rededication to be repeated until he came again. Jesus gave no direc-
tions as to frequency, ritual to be observed, or explanation of meaning;
but he and his men had been eating together when he took up bread,
broke it, and passed it round, commenting that it "was" his body, and
then passed wine, commenting that it was the blood of a new covenant, poured out for the forgiveness of sins. Paul tells the Corinthian
church that Jesus also said, "This do, as often as you drink it, in remembrance of me." There is some reason to think that this simple pattern was followed whenever disciples ate together. They would find it
a poignant reminder of that last meal with Jesus. For all Christians
since it has provided a perpetual rendezvous with the risen Christ,
with a vivid recalling of his death for us.

According to John's Gospel, it was at this "communion table"
that Jesus gave another firm instruction for the future, the new commandment that disciples love one another. Judas had just departed to
betray Jesus, the first breach in the disciple band, and Jesus insists at
once on the mutual loyalty necessary to any future effectiveness. A little later he insists also that the disciples must abide in him, as branches
in the vine, if they are to bear any fruit for God, the vinedresser. Earlier (according to Matthew) Jesus had given counsel on the dangers of
disunity by urging that any occasions of offense between brethren

should be dealt with seriously and directly — first one-to-one, then if necessary by two or three to one, and if still necessary, by the whole church.

In this pastoral concern it is noteworthy that Jesus emphasizes special care for the immature convert. Further, Jesus promised that decisions reached unitedly would be ratified in heaven and prayers offered unitedly would be answered by the Father (Matt. 18:10-14, 15-19; compare John 21:16). For this continuing unity Jesus himself prayed "that they all may be one" on the night before his death, the defection of Judas being again in his mind (John 17:11, 12, 21). In all this it is plain that Jesus anticipated that future disciples would share corporate life and service, not a merely individual loyalty. Leadership for the future church fell almost inevitably to those with experience of life with Christ, who could testify to seeing the risen Lord (Acts 1:21ff.). Thus "apostle" ("sent one, envoy") was early applied to the Twelve (Matthias replacing Judas), to Paul (who had seen Jesus risen), to James the Lord's brother (to whom Jesus appeared), to Barnabas, and possibly to others. Other brethren of Jesus also attained prominence, probably on grounds of family and faith (Acts 1:14, 1 Cor. 9:5). Nothing is said of "ordination," other than "as the Father has sent me so I send you," which applies to all Christians. Neither is anything said of priesthood, and in view of the qualifications required nothing could be said of successors.

Peter had been promised "the keys of the kingdom of heaven" and "whatever you shall bind . . . [or] loose . . . on earth shall be bound . . . [or] loosed . . . in heaven" (Matt. 16:19ff.). A steward or manager of a large household held the keys in his own hands, opening the door to visitors, closing it against intruders. Peter, it would seem, by his confession of Christ's messiahship and sonship has opened the door of the kingdom to all future comers. We may think this fulfilled at Pentecost. "Binding" and "loosing" were current technical terms for legal and ethical decisions. Peter is not recorded to have exercised such responsibility; James, Christ's brother, presided over the church council of Jerusalem (Acts 15). Again, nothing at all is said of any successor to Peter.

Indeed, Jesus sternly warns that questions of status must not arise among these "friends" of his, or toward newer disciples. "The scribes and the Pharisees . . . bind heavy burdens, hard to bear, and lay them on men's shoulders. . . . They make their phylacteries [text-boxes bound with ribbon on hand and brow] broad and their fringes [tassels attached to a shawl or cape, originally as signs of obedience to divine law] long." They occupy seats of honor at feasts and in synagogues and "love salutations in the market places, and being called rabbi [teacher] by men." Here are all the titles, claims, and trappings of spiritual status, superiority, and authority; here too is the sharp injunction to leaders in Christ's future church: "You are not to be called rabbi, for you have one teacher, and you are all brethren. And call no man your father on earth, for you have one Father, who is in heaven. Neither be called masters, for you have one master, the Christ. He who is greatest among you shall be your servant . . ." (Matt. 23:1ff.). Bearing witness, serving in Christ's name and in his way needs no uniform, no titles, no adulation, no public claim to religious "authority."

The Christian missioner is authorized to accept hospitality and maintenance: "The laborer deserves his food. . . . Whatever town or village you enter, find out who is worthy in it, and stay with him until you depart" (Matt. 10:8-11). But his ministry must not be traded: as he has received without paying, so he must give without payment. It should be added that, just as increasing numbers made Christian buildings a practical necessity (though not for luxurious architectural display), so changing circumstances created the need for training in ministry and scholarship in faithful interpretation. As the centuries passed, the faithful were more and more removed from the original history, languages, and documents of the faith, as well as from the ancient contention with rival religions and philosophies. Later generations of church leaders needed something more than a sincere witness to spiritual experience. But Jesus' demand that no believers presume to dominate over their brothers and sisters remains paramount. In Christ's church as Jesus describes it, authority belongs to Christ alone.

One other instruction that Jesus bequeathed was a solemn warning to expect hostility. The missioners were sent "as sheep among wolves"; henceforth they will be hated of all men for Christ's sake, "as they hated him." In the world they will have tribulation. The basic reason for that antipathy is the clear and deliberate difference of life-style between Christ's followers and others, the different values trea-sured, the different ethical judgments implied. "If you were of the world, the world would love its own; but because you are not of the world . . . therefore the world hates you." Disciples must not seek ma-terial things "as Gentiles do," nor pray " as heathen do," nor take oaths "as the irreverent do." Again and again Jesus uses the words "it shall not be so among you."

This difference between the church and non-Christian society is, to Jesus' mind, of the essence of the church and must not be ignored or compromised to win popular acceptance or converts. The salt of the earth must not lose its savor, nor the light of Christian truth be hid in some "bushel" of obscure jargon. Yet the church must live within society, paying its dues to competent authorities (Matt. 17:27), serv-ing, teaching, healing, befriending, never returning hostility with abuse or contempt. Nothing in Jesus' teaching or example suggests the kind of withdrawal from society, whether communal or solitary, that developed later, even though largely in self-defense.

Finally, Jesus left to his church two far-reaching promises that lift the whole ecclesiastical story to transcendent levels. In view of the church's faults, divisions, confusions, failures, and sins, it requires a considerable effort of faith to accept that she is not a wholly human institution. Yet Jesus promised, "Where two or three are gathered in my name, *there am I* in the midst of them"; "Lo, I am with you always, to the close of the age" (Matt. 18:20, 28:20). And there are sufficient remarkable things about the church — her survival at all, after centu-ries of persecution, her self-reformation, her extension through the world, her power of adjustment to many different cultures, her tenac-ity of faith, her ability to kindle selflessness and saintliness in humble people — to persuade us that in spite of all that we regret, there is in-spiration, power, and vision more than human that sustains her.

This promise focuses upon the presence in the church of the Spirit who came upon Jesus at his baptism and later upon the whole church at Pentecost, endlessly enabling, equipping, reviving the church through the ages. In a world believed to be dominated by evil spirits, the promise of the *Holy* Spirit's presence and power available to faith at all times was especially reassuring. Yet the Spirit *is* "the Spirit of Jesus" (Acts 16:6, 7, 2 Cor. 3:17, Phil. 1:19), and as Jesus repeated in the Upper Room, speaking of his "departure": "I will pray the Father, and he will give you another Counselor, to be with you for ever, even the Spirit of truth . . . ; you know him, for he dwells with you, and will be in you." . . . "He will teach you . . . bear witness . . . convince the world . . . guide into all truth . . . show you coming things," so gathering up the past and leading into the future. Sometimes the church has sought "manifestations" of the Spirit which Jesus never promised; but the abiding power and ministry of the Spirit of Jesus still preserves the church — and will do so.

That is the other far-reaching promise that Jesus left to his church: "the gates of Hades shall not prevail against it." The language is unclear, because "Hades" sometimes means the abode of evil spirits and sometimes "death" (the Hebrew "Sheol"; in Ps. 9:13 "the throes of death"?). Christ's own resurrection, being "loosed" from the pangs of death "because it was not possible for him to be held by it" (Acts 2:24), parallels the implication of the church's victory over death and hell at the last.

This is true, of course, not of every individual Christian church, each subject to circumstances, shifts of population, its own faithfulness or spiritual decline, but of the church Jesus describes, his agency in the earth, the reincarnation of his Spirit. No local church is immortal; even the great church at Ephesus was warned of removal if she did not recover her first love. But the church as Christ described her is immortal, and invulnerable, and shall prevail, even in a "post-Christian" age.

So Jesus promised.

II

Jesus on the Place of Women in Religion and Society

"CHRIST'S ATTITUDE to women has altered their position in the world." That statement has ample authority behind it, but to appreciate its truth it is necessary to consider the cultural situation that Jesus faced.

In Jewry in New Testament times (despite some contrary trends in the Old Testament) women were constantly discriminated against in religion as firmly as in society.

(a) On the basis of the Eden story, women were blamed for all the evil in the world.

(b) In synagogue they were segregated and silenced, allowed to overhear but not to take part in discussion (compare 1 Cor. 14:34-35). At the Temple they were confined to the Women's Court.

(c) Speaking with women in public places was frowned upon; strict Pharisees would not converse with their wives or daughters in public.

(d) Unlike men, women had no right of divorce.

(e) Women were ritually "unclean" at various times: after childbirth, wholly unclean for seven days and partially so for a further thirty-three days, both periods doubled if the child was a girl; and after any sexual event for fixed times.

(f) Women's testimony was not valid in any court or in business matters.

(g) Women received no formal or legal education. From about 75 BC, elementary education was "compulsory" for Jewish boys, "girls being still restricted to the tuition of the home." As to religious education, some rabbis held it wasted effort to teach women the law, while others counted it actually mischievous. "Better to burn the precepts of the law than to teach them to a woman" is one recorded opinion. The pious Jew included in his synagogue prayer thanksgiving that God had not made him a woman.

It is astonishing to notice how deliberately, even relentlessly, Jesus set himself to oppose this discrimination, point by point.

(a) Jesus never once referred to the Eden story, or to Eve's part in it, in explanation of human sin or mortality.

(b) Jesus never once in his public speaking to assembled guests, to crowds on the hillsides or by the sea, separated women from men in any promise he made, any instruction given, any invitation offered, in the terms of discipleship, in describing God's kingdom, counseling about prayer, promising to send the Spirit, *or anything else.* Paul perfectly defined the attitude of Jesus: "In Christ there is . . . neither male nor female, for you are all one in Christ Jesus" (Gal. 3:28).

(c) With his mother at Cana, with Martha at Lazarus's tomb, with the woman "taken in adultery," the woman who "washed his feet with tears," another who anointed them with perfume, with the woman at the garden tomb, the woman who hailed him from the crowd, and those who sympathized with his suffering, Jesus spoke without hesitation or restraint. At his talking with the woman at Jacob's well his own disciples were shocked, not because she was a Samaritan, but because "he was talking with a woman," yet none asked, "Why are you talking with her?" Their silence is significant.

(d) Moses' requirement that men divorcing their wives must give the wife a certificate of divorcement to arm her against any future conjugal or financial claims had come to be regarded as implying permission to divorce, and it belonged to men only. Contemporary rabbis argued the terms of such divorce, accepting the male privilege. Jesus declared it merely a safeguard against "the hardness of men's hearts," and against the custom he appealed to the original divine intention, that man and wife should become one, as permanently and inarguably as the union with their parents which by marrying they were leaving. That divine intention applied of course to the wife as well as to the husband (Matt. 19:3ff.).

(e) The supposed "uncleanness" from contact with women Jesus simply ignored. One, unclean from her ailment, touched his garment from behind; he turned to comfort her. Another, unclean by reputation, did for him the kindly service of a hostess. The neglectful host privately concluded that Jesus could not be a prophet since he let such a woman touch him. Jesus defended her from criticism with almost violent indignation, comforting her meanwhile. The Syrophoenician woman was unclean, being gentile; Jesus granted her prayer nonetheless. And he took by the hand the apparently dead child of Jairus. In all such cases the question of uncleanness simply did not arise for Jesus. As to any uncleanness attaching to childbearing, Jesus set himself firmly against any idea that children are born in sin or sinful in life because "they were born like it" (if that is what the author of Psalm 51 meant). He declared unequivocally that "to such belongs the kingdom of heaven," adding "see that you do not despise one of these little ones."

(f) Again, women's testimony became with Jesus not only valid but all-important. When the angels sent Mary Magdalene and Joanna, Mary the mother of James, and other women to tell the apostles that Jesus was risen, the men dismissed their testimony as idle talk. But Jesus himself commissioned Mary Magdalene and "the other Mary" to "go and tell my brethren" the most glorious testimony ever uttered. By women.

(g) As to religious education, women received Jesus' instruction equally with men: "certain women who had followed him from Galilee, who stood at a distance" in the end to watch him die; other "women who had been healed of evil spirits and infirmities: Mary called Magdalene, . . . and Joanna the wife of Chuza, Herod's steward, and Susanna, and many others, who provided for [the Twelve] out of their means." Women were among the five thousand Jesus fed after a day's teaching; still others heard his expressed compassion for "the daughters of Jerusalem." It is true no woman was appointed among the Twelve; propriety alone prevented that, as the disciple group traveled the lonely roads, sleeping on the hillsides, bathing and washing clothes in streams. (That Jesus was careful of such considerations is evident from John 4:16 — if evidence is needed.)

On this last issue, one incident preserved by Luke takes on immense significance. At supper in Bethany, Martha busies herself with lavish preparations while Mary listens to Jesus. At this, Martha complains. With gentle playfulness Jesus urges that one item of food will be sufficient, and Mary has already chosen her supper — her "good portion" — to listen and learn. Perhaps deliberately, Luke uses the same phrase about Mary that he uses later in Acts for Paul's *"sitting at the feet"* of Gamaliel, his famous tutor. It was the customary phrase to describe a student's relation to his teacher. There is little doubt that Mary symbolizes, for Luke, the new figure introduced by Christianity, the woman deliberately instructed in religion, whose opportunity (Jesus says) "shall not be taken away from her."

It is plainly not enough to say, negatively, that Jesus himself did not discriminate in any way against women. We must add that positively, of set purpose, he actively opposed the prevailing discrimination, and set women in equal status with men in the kingdom of God.

Jesus' actions confirm his words. The Gospels *name* at least fifteen women in Jesus' story, and mention women nearly forty times, often at important points such as Jesus' birth, his presentation in the Temple, his boyhood obedience to Mary, his necessary but painful detachment from home (at Cana's wedding), the women he healed, the homes opened to him, one who anointed him for burial, another who declared his mother blessed in such a son, the women holding vigil at the cross, the attention of women to his burial rites and at his resurrection. Certain other incidents place Jesus' high valuation of women beyond question.

Hindered at the city gate of Nain by a funeral procession, Jesus learned that the deceased was the only son of a widow. Luke's story concentrates on that woman: "When the Lord saw her, he had compassion on her and said to her, 'Do not weep.' . . . the dead man sat up. . . . And [Jesus] gave him to his mother." Similarly, Jesus watched wealthy worshipers make their gifts to the Temple treasury and noticed — again — "a poor widow" who put in two copper coins. He commented, "Truly I tell you, this poor widow has put in *more than all* of them. For they all contributed out of their abundance, but she out of her poverty put in all the living that she had." The assessment of gifts by the resources available is striking; so is Jesus' notice of the woman behind the gift. We recall that Jesus' mother was widowed, and not wealthy; he knew the signs.

Jesus was on the very frontier of the holy land, wishing not to be known, when a Gentile woman, a Syrophoenician, kneeling before him, weeping, begged healing for her daughter. Jesus was silent, and impatient disciples besought him to send her away. Jesus replied, "I am not sent but to the lost sheep of the house of Israel." This is precisely the limitation which he had set on the mission of the Twelve: "Go nowhere among the Gentiles . . . go rather to the lost sheep of the house of Israel." To the woman's further pleading, Jesus replied, "It is not meet to take the children's bread and throw it to dogs" — "dogs" being the Jewish epithet for Gentiles. Taking up Jesus' word, the woman replied, "Yes, Lord, yet even the dogs eat the crumbs that fall from their master's table." So Matthew tells it; Mark says that Jesus prefaced the words "It is not meet" with "Let the children first be fed," and gives Jesus' final words as "For this saying you may go your way; the demon has left your daughter."

The suggestion that Jesus' hesitation was in order to test her faith is not in the story, and quite unlike Jesus' usual response to a distraught mother and a daughter "suffering terribly" (NIV) at home. It is obvious that Jesus changed his mind, changed too the range of his ministry. Thereafter Jesus spoke of "Wherever the gospel is preached in the whole world . . . Go therefore and make disciples of all nations . . . Repentance and forgiveness should be preached to all nations . . . Other sheep I have which are not of this fold. . . ." As if to illustrate this wider range, Jesus returned from the border area through Decapolis, a region of Galilee mainly Greek.

The cause of this change of mind and range, according to Matthew, was the woman's faith. We know that Jesus had "marveled" at the great faith he found in a Gentile centurion, saying "Not even in Israel have I found such faith." According to Mark, the cause was her "saying," about household dogs eating unwanted crumbs from the children's table. These are exactly the two reasons that led the later church to welcome Gentiles into membership, Peter stressing that God cleansed Gentiles' hearts by faith (Acts 15:7ff., 10:43 — spoken to Gentiles); and Paul arguing that when Jews refuse the gospel (letting it fall from their table!) then Gentiles have their opportunity (Acts 13:46ff., 18:6, Rom. 11:7-11). Can this be mere coincidence?

At least we can say that this story was deeply pondered in apostolic days. But are we faced with the possibility that Jesus himself heard a word from the Father through this Gentile's lips, kindling even for him a wider vision? In his temptation Jesus thought out different ways of building his kingdom; as his ministry developed he saw himself more like the promised Servant of the Lord than Son of David the warrior-king. It is not impossible that he began by understanding God's kingdom as essentially Jewish and came to see it as God's purpose for all mankind when Jews rejected his message. We know that Jesus listened constantly to his Father's leading. Might it not be that one woman's faith and wit had its place in kindling that universal vision? The early church thought so.

It was to a woman that Jesus paid the highest compliment and made a most far-reaching promise. She had broken over him a jar of costly perfume, sensing (while the men still argued who should be greatest in the kingdom) that Jesus was about to die. When the men looked askance, Jesus said, "She has done a *beautiful* thing to me," adding "wherever the gospel is preached in the whole world, what she has done will be told in memory of her." She was, after all, at that moment the only individual in the whole world who saw, felt, understood what Jesus was thinking and suffering. "She has anointed my body beforehand for burying," he said. "Let her alone" was surely spoken, not to the caviling disciples alone, but to Judaism — and to the coming church.

Finally, there is Luke's wonderfully significant story of the woman "who had a spirit of infirmity for eighteen years; she was bent over and could not fully straighten herself." She is the very caricature of Jewish women in society and religion — "whom Satan bound" is Jesus' ruthless comment. Jesus called her and said, "Woman, you are freed from your infirmity." Of course there was controversy; it was the Sabbath, and religious rules were more important than eighteen years of suffering. Jesus was indignant; his reply — that these hypocrites would readily *unbind* their ox or ass on the Sabbath for watering — was unanswerable; and the woman went forth from the synagogue to a totally new experience, upright, fearless, able to look men and women in the face, and free. That is Luke's vivid illustration of what Jesus and the gospel were doing for women throughout that Roman world.

It is no accident that so many of the above utterances and reminiscences of Jesus come from Luke's Gospel. Luke, a Gentile, was familiar with the situation of women in pagan society: sometimes honored, even worshiped, but often degraded as slaves, exploited as devotees of Aphrodite and in the city slums of the empire. He is writing to inform His Excellency Theophilus (a Roman official of probably equestrian rank; compare Luke 1:3, Acts 1:1 with Acts 23:26, 24:2) about the new Christian movement spreading through the world. His books show concern with social problems — wealth, peace, race relations, religious rivalries, and the place of women in the state — such as a provincial governor would need to deal with. Luke has seen in the church, while traveling with Paul, a tenderness, dignity, equality, and opportunity accorded to women that contrasted sharply with contemporary custom. He continues therefore his emphasis upon women's place in Christianity in the story in Acts as the church moved out into that pagan world. Women gather with the apostles in the home of Mary after Christ's ascension; the Spirit falls at Pentecost upon "daughters and handmaidens"; four daughters of Philip are prophetesses in the church; widows serve the church at Jerusalem; Dorcas is full of good works; women share in persecution at Damascus; Lydia (and a pythoness) help form the church at Philippi; Priscilla is the gifted teacher of Apollos; Rhoda, Damaris, with "leading women" of Thessalonica, Greek women of high standing at Berea — all are part of the new Christian society as Luke describes it. In Christ a new era had indeed dawned for women, offering liberation, equal value in God's sight, wide social and religious vocation — and Luke would have His Excellency Theophilus know it.

Christ's attitude to women has indeed signaled a change in their position in the world. Strictly speaking, that change began just before the birth of Jesus, when an obscure village maid burst into exultant poetry:

> My soul doth magnify the Lord,
> And my spirit hath rejoiced in God my Saviour.
> For he hath regarded the low estate of his handmaiden:
> For, behold, from henceforth all generations shall call me blessed.
> For He that is mighty hath done to me great things,
>   And holy is his name. (KJV)

12

Jesus in a Racist Climate

To SEE JESUS always against the background of first-century Judaism is necessary but insufficient. His society was riven by racial, nationalist, "fundamentalist" antagonisms as bitter as any in the modern world. The familiar comment in John's Gospel, whether we understand it as "Jews have no dealings with Samaritans" (John 4:9, RSV) or as the very apposite "Jews and Samaritans do not use drinking vessels in common," states their mutual antipathy very mildly, as from distant hindsight. During Jesus' time the mutual enmity was deep and often violent, fuelled by unforgiving memories of long-past history, by nationalist claims and ambitions, and by profound religious fervor, dogmatically contending for rigid religious ideas.

Not long before Jesus' birth, some reckless Samaritans, finding the Jerusalem temple gates open at night to accommodate the hosts of festal pilgrims, burst in and "threw about dead bodies in the cloisters," as Josephus, the first-century Jewish historian expressed it. As a result, Samaritans were excluded from such occasions thereafter. A few years later, the murder of a Galilean on his way down the Samaritan road to Jerusalem led to a vengeful party leaving the religious festival to confront a Samaritan force. Many were killed; an appeal to Caesar was followed by several crucifixions and the replacement of inefficient Roman officials.

The root causes of this relentless antagonism were those familiar also in our time. Samaritans envied Judea's wealth, religious importance, and political power; they resented having Romans and Galileans encroach upon their territory, if only to cross it by the quickest road from north to south for military or religious purposes. For their part, Jews could not forget that when the "northern kingdom" of Israel was exiled to Assyria in the eighth century B.C., the vacated territory was repeopled with ethnic groups from Babylonia and Syria, who eventually intermarried with the Israelite peasants left behind. The descendants of this racial and religious mixture were the Samaritans. To a people as proud of their pure descent and divine election as the Jews, such a barbarous origin was contemptible. Even a noble teacher like Ben Sirach, some two centuries B.C., could write:

Two nations my soul detests
    And the third is not even a people;
Those who live in Seir, and the Philistines,
    And the foolish people who live in Shechem. (50:25)

The prophet Hosea, likewise, describes the state of Samaritan society in a brusque phrase: "the wicked deeds of Samaria" (7:1, 8:5, 10:5, 13:16).

Such a history gave ample ground for later Jews to assume that Samaritans in general were indeed "fools" in religion: heretics, compromisers, and syncretists. The bitterness was heightened rather than assuaged by the many claims Samaria could make to the original sites, relics, and stories of Israel's religion.

At Shechem, it was said, Joshua himself had recited the great acts of God that had brought Israel to Canaan; there he established the covenant between God and his people (Joshua 24); there they buried the bones of the great Joseph; there Jacob himself dug a well the Samaritans still used; and there he buried the "household images" that Rachel had stolen from Laban. In Samaria was a field reputedly given by Jacob to Joseph; to Shechem Rehoboam had rallied the northern tribes in revolt against the south; Shechem was among the favored "cities of refuge." Samaria contained Shiloh, original home of the sacred Ark and closely associated with Eli the priest and Samuel the prophet and kingmaker. Mount Gerizim, where (as Samaritans claimed) Abraham had offered up Isaac, became the site of the great temple that survived for two centuries. No wonder, then, that Samaritans could speak familiarly of "Jacob our father" (John 4:12), and revile "upstart" Judah whose importance dated only from David and Solomon.

Judah reciprocated this attitude with interest, not merely by ostracizing the Samaritans from all social intercourse but by accusing them of willful heresy, of neglect of the Mosaic law they claimed to observe, of immorality of all kinds, and of maintaining close relations with the world of evil spirits.

How did Jesus react to this mutual bitterness?

The accusation that Samaritans cooperated with demons underlies the charge against Jesus that he was a Samaritan and had a demon (John 8:48). One Jewish "mystical" interpretation of the Aramaic word for "Samaritan" changed the vowels to reveal a hidden name for Satan! As Mark shows, Jesus dealt very seriously with the dangerous suggestion that he was in league with the devil (3:22-30). He teaches that whoever cannot distinguish works that are divine from those that are devilish is placing himself beyond forgiveness; to reject the light of the Spirit of truth is to make repentance impossible, and pardon therefore out of reach. But the charge that he was a Samaritan Jesus merely ignored.

This accusation clearly exposes the tense racist and religious bitterness within which Jesus' ministry was set. So does the refusal of a Samaritan village to provide lodging for Jesus on his way southward: "the people would not receive him because his face was set toward Jerusalem" (Luke 9:51). The disciples' reaction, "Lord, do you want us to bid fire come down from heaven and consume them?" combines typical Jewish antagonism with a hint of scriptural justification in Elijah's destruction of a hundred soldiers in somewhat similar circumstances (2 Kings 1:9). A specific reference to Elijah and Jesus' reply "You do not know what manner of spirit you are of, for the Son of man came not to destroy men's lives but to save them," do not appear in the oldest copies of Luke. They seem to be either sound Christian comment — or possibly additional oral testimony — added in later copies. Certainly Jesus rebuked the proposal — "and they went on to another village." Again Jesus ignored the Samaritan-versus-Jew issue involved.

The initial reaction of the Samaritan woman to Jesus' request for water (John 4) similarly reflects the automatic recoil of Samaritan from Jew: "How is it that you, a Jew, ask a drink of me, a woman of Samaria?" And Jesus once again ignores the implied hostility. Indeed, Jesus himself appears to anticipate such a reaction when, early in his ministry, at his first sending out the disciples on a widespread mission, he advises them to confine their attention to Jews: "enter no town of the Samaritans" (Matt. 10:5). This reads like temporary counsel to beginners, in view of prevailing attitudes; by the end of his ministry Jesus speaks of "other sheep" he must bring to God's fold, besides Jews, and commissions his now matured disciples to make new disciples "of all nations," Samaria being specifically mentioned after "Jerusalem and all Judea" before "the end of the earth" (Matt. 28:19, Acts 1:8).

In all these instances Jesus' policy may be described as the avoidance of confrontation when racist or nationalist issues are raised. But on three occasions Jesus' response to this seething situation was deliberately positive, even (as coming from a Jew) in Jewish eyes provocative. Journeying "between Samaria and Galilee" (Luke 17:11ff.), Jesus was met by a group of ten lepers who pleaded for his compassion. Jesus sent them, as Jewish law required, to the priests who alone could declare them healed and safe to return to society. One, excited to find himself cured, returned to Jesus loudly praising God, and falling before Jesus poured out his thanksgiving. Deliberately, Jesus drew attention to the absence of the other nine: "Was no one found to return and give praise to God except this foreigner?" — for the pious, grateful man in the group was a Samaritan. It was only a remark, but it expressed a telling judgment that neither the disciples nor any Jewish by-standers would welcome.

Second, answering a Jewish lawyer's loaded question about inher-iting eternal life, Jesus made him recite the commandment to love God and one's neighbor. The lawyer, "desiring to justify himself," asked the crucial, tendentious question, "And who is my neighbor?" He received in reply the famous parable about one who showed gener-ous kindness to a chance-met victim on the road. So Jesus made *the lawyer* say who was "neighbor" in such a situation, and dismissed his questioner with "Go, and do likewise." But the sharp, disturbing, and, in Jewish ears, provocative detail in the parable lay in making the shin-ing example of good neighborliness, fulfilling the great command-ment of Jewish law, a Samaritan — and in making the lawyer himself admit it!

But Jesus' most compelling challenge to contemporary attitudes in this respect was his deliberate (and again in Jewish eyes provocative) mission to Samaria (John 4). Entering Samaritan territory as far as Ja-cob's well, near Sychar and not far from the capital, Shechem, Jesus without hesitation or fuss broke through four taboos at once: that which forbade a Jew to seek help of any but a fellow-Jew; that which frowned upon any man conversing with a woman in public; that which discouraged any Jewish-Samaritan conversation at all; and that which forbade a Jew to use a Samaritan's food vessel. He asked a Sa-maritan woman for a drink. Without even noticing her challenging question he humbly urged his need. Few attitudes are more immedi-ately conciliatory. Something very deliberate was afoot.

With the desired drink as text Jesus discoursed on the "living wa-ter" that quenches still deeper thirst and springs up within the soul to eternal life. He emphasizes that this gift is for *whoever* drinks: Jews, Sa-maritans, or others. When she would pursue the theme, apparently with limited understanding, Jesus suggests that she bring her husband, perhaps for propriety's sake, though the effect is to reveal her unhappy domestic situation. This convinces the woman that Jesus is a prophet, such as Amos, Hosea, or Elijah, who once ministered in northern Israel. So she raises the sharpest religious issue between Jew and Samaritan: which was the true, the one divinely appointed temple for God's dwelling and worship, that in Jerusalem or the more ancient shrine on Mount Gerizim?

To this Jesus makes the revolutionary reply that *neither* is the true place of worship: "the hour is coming when neither on this mountain nor in Jerusalem will you worship the Father." That was startling in the current situation. Jesus added that the Samaritans had something more to learn of God, just as he would certainly say of Jews: but "the hour is coming, and now is, when the true worshipers will worship the Father in spirit and truth" wherever they worship, the sincerity being more important than the place. Moreover, "the Father *seeks* such" whether Jew or Samaritan, "to worship him." Even the repetition of "the Father" is significant. Jesus is avoiding terms like "God of Israel," "God of the covenant," even "God of our fathers": he speaks of the creator, God and Father of all.

To this surprising assertion the woman replies that when Messiah comes he will explain all such mysteries, for Samaritans, too, cherished a messianic hope. But Jesus startles further by asserting "I that speak to you am he" — Messiah of Jews and Samaritans alike.

This is a concept of religion that passes all racial and national frontiers. Neither God himself nor acceptable worship is confined to any one race or temple or traditional form. So long as worship is offered in spirit and in truth it is acceptable on high. Access to God, response to his seeking, like the water of life, is for whoever will. The woman returned to her neighbors with glowing heart and thrilling testimony of her encounter.

Meanwhile, Jesus revealed his own heart's response to the interview by speaking of the invigorating spiritual food to be found in doing God's work and will, and emphasizing the readiness for harvest of the widespread fields of mission already there before them in the great plain of Samaria.

Jesus' words were quickly verified, as "many Samaritans from that city believed on him because of the woman's testimony. . . . Many more believed because of his word." And they clamored for him to stay with them.

The Samaritan mission lasted only a further two days, but it was one of Jesus' most successful visits to any area. The truth preached there was among the most profound and far-reaching of his teaching, aptly summarized in the Samaritans' confession that Jesus is "indeed the savior *of the world*" — a concept the Jews had never entertained. The ultimate historic importance of the event was revealed in the welcome Samaria afforded to Christians fleeing persecution at Jerusalem, and the remarkable response of Samaria to the mission of Philip, when "multitudes with one accord gave heed to what was said, and many were healed," so that Peter and John were sent by the Jerusalem church to investigate and confirm the Samaritan "revival" (Acts 8:1, 5ff.).

But the full significance of Jesus' evangelization of Samaria is understood only if we keep in mind the sharp racist and nationalist situation and the deep and lasting offense that such a mission to Samaritans, by one claiming to be Messiah, would cause to orthodox Jews. Perhaps all the more shocking because the two-day mission, like the healing of the leper, was initiated by Samaritan invitation.

What then may be learned from Jesus for our time?

No recorded saying shows Jesus either promoting or pursuing any discussion of the issues or root causes involved in this perpetual antagonism. The nearest Jesus approaches to such comes in his remarks provocative to his fellow Jews but in favor of Samaritan gratitude, good neighborliness, and readiness for "harvest." The one similar remark on the other side is the reminder, in Samaria, that "salvation is of the Jews," but *for* all. Nothing like persistent argument, propaganda, baiting, or theological point-scoring ever occurs. Apparently Jesus would treat all such "religious" argumentation as futile and destructive.

Nor did Jesus tolerate any retaliation. He ignored test-questions, accusations, and active rejection; responding in kind prolongs enmity. Jesus did not appeal to the universal law of eastern hospitality from unwilling hosts. Yet he remained open to the invitation to heal, remain, teach, even asking favors — each a simple but valuable example to ourselves. And he recognized good *wherever* it is found.

Behind all is the vision of a worship that God accepts — and seeks — which relies not upon place, ritual, hierarchy, or tradition but upon spirit and truth alone, because God seeks such equally everywhere, offering eternal life to "whoever" will accept. For Jesus is the Savior not of Jews, Samaritans, or Christians only, but of the world, which God loves.

This is hardly a program of action to defeat the racist and nationalist antagonisms that have bedeviled land after land through the twentieth century. Much practical, even political, thought and action are required to even begin to frame such a program. But the mind and example of Jesus, and his call to follow it, will prove essential in the end if ever the world peace we seek is to be realized.

13

Jesus on God — and Godliness

J ESUS' MOST FREQUENT name for God, "Father," though essentially a
figure of speech (since God has neither wife nor family), endows
"the eternal," "the first cause" with personality, character, relationship,
and benevolence. Yet this divine name was not original, but one which
Jews often heard in synagogue readings of scripture: "[God is] a father
of the fatherless"; "As a father pities his children, so the LORD pities
those who fear him"; "Have we not all one father?"; "Thou art our Father, though Abraham does not know us and Israel does not acknowledge us; thou, O LORD, art our Father. . . ."

This Old Testament background of the title must not be forgot-
ten, for the Jewish father was not the indulgent parent sometimes
imagined, but both ruler and priest of the family. Jesus sometimes
adds "in heaven," "heavenly Father," "Holy Father," "Righteous Father," "My Father," "Father, Lord of heaven and earth" to remind us
that the Father is also, and nonetheless, God. Though he was closer to
God than we can ever be, Jesus yet taught us to say "Our Father" and
spoke to "my brethren" about "my Father and your Father." John's
Gospel refers to God as "the Father" some one hundred twelve times,
so thoroughly had that title entered Christianity by the close of the
century.

Jesus could also speak of "the Most High," and emphasize that God has never been seen by men, is timeless (the God of succeeding generations), and self-existent ("has life in himself"). Thus the later apostolic description of the Christians' God as "the God and Father of our Lord Jesus Christ" is most apt.

Jesus' use of this Old Testament title underlines his awareness of the place God held in the history of his people. In the same way, Jesus inherited the vivid awareness of the place of God in the world of nature which runs through poet (Job), psalmist, and prophet. Israel's world is full of God: "the earth is the LORD's . . . ; for he has founded it upon the seas, and established it upon the rivers"; "Thou didst cleave open springs and brooks . . . Thine is the day, thine also the night; thou hast established the luminaries and the sun . . . thou hast made summer and winter"; "The earth is full of the steadfast love of the LORD." In the remarkable words of Job, "If God should take back his spirit to himself, and gather to himself his breath, all flesh would perish together, and man would return to dust."

Just so did Jesus see the whole physical world as God's, sustained by God, ruled by God as of right, and wholly dependent upon God's providence all the time. Challenged for working on the Sabbath, Jesus replied, "My Father is working still, and I work."

Some Jewish teachers held that at creation God rested on the seventh day but did not cease to work. "As the property of fire is to burn and of snow to chill, so the property of God is to create," said the Jewish teacher Philo. The sun rises, rivers flow, babes are born, fruit ripens, living things grow, all on the Sabbath, without breaking the Sabbath, "for the whole world is God's private residence."

So Jesus says, it is God who "makes his sun rise on the evil and on the good, and sends rain on the just and on the unjust" — reading God's character from natural phenomena. It is God who "clothes the grass," "adorns the lilies," "gives us our daily bread," "knows what we need before we ask him," "counts the hairs upon our heads," "feeds the ravens," "observes the falling sparrow." It is God who instituted and protected human marriage and who will judge severely any who harm little children. So closely involved is "the most High God" in the welfare of the natural, everyday world; to speak of the Father as "in heaven" most emphatically does not imply, for Jesus, that he is not also abroad in the earth.

As we saw, this "fatherhood" ascribed to God enshrines the truth of his universal goodwill, omniscient, generous, individual, protective, redemptive, always dependable. It confirms the "steadfast love" so very often asserted of God in the Old Testament, and affirms a second "property" of God, to love whatever he has created. Jesus continually analyzes this divine goodwill: the Father may be trusted to provide what is needful, to give good things to those who ask him, to protect our souls as necessary with additional moral strength (for "no one shall pluck [Christ's own] out of the Father's hands," and "it is not the will of the Father that any should perish"). The Father will answer our petitions, send us the Spirit to guide us into all truth needed for discipleship, give us the true bread that nourishes spiritual life, and receive believers at last into the Father's house.

Such love is offered to all who will receive it. But God never invades the freedom with which he has endowed human personality, and man may shut himself out of love. It is interesting to notice, in Jesus' famous parable of the prodigal son, that the father lets the rebellious son go and leaves him unsought in the far country, although (like God) he watches eagerly for the penitent's return. Especially does Jesus assure us that "the Father himself loves" the followers of Jesus, and at the service of that love "all things are possible with God" (Matt. 19:26).

Certainly, in Jesus' thought there is nothing maudlin or sentimental about this emphasis upon divine love, not only because God is King as well as Father but also because there is room for fear as well as faith in our relation to him. God, we must ever remember, "seeth in secret," "can destroy both body and soul in hell," and sets standards very different from men's: "what is exalted among men is an abomination in the sight of God" (Luke 16:15). He can refuse to forgive the unforgiving and even cancel forgiveness already given (Matt. 18:32ff.).

God's love is not to be trifled with, after all: no wonder it could be said that we know God best through Christ's plain and penetrating insights (John 14:7-9).

Our relationship to God our Father must involve "things that belong to God," which, Jesus says, "must be rendered" as rightly due from us as any things that belong to Caesar. Life in God's inward kingdom is an immense privilege, given us by "the Father's good pleasure," but it has its obligations, the first of which is to "love the Lord your God with all your heart, and with all your soul, and with all your mind." There can be no sharing this devotion with other objects — with the search for wealth ("mammon"), ambition, fame, or other rival idolatries. God does ask an undivided devotion. And from an undivided personality; not from desire, emotion, profession, or an intellect at war with itself, but one united in the supreme aim of glorifying God and serving his purposes.

In response to God's assurances and promises the only fitting attitude is trust, the quiet confidence or "faith" that will not let the heart be troubled because it relies upon God's faithfulness. The expression and the nourishment of such faith is worship, which "the Father seeks" not in any particular place or form ("Samaria" or "Jerusalem") but in spirit and in truth. Gratitude, aspiration, and praise combine to honor God, even as Jesus himself "honored" the Father (John 8:49). Such repeated acknowledgment of divine claims upon us is one sure way to spiritual progress, maturity of character, and deeper insight.

The voice of trust and the vehicle of worship is prayer, which Jesus urges should rise from the secret places of the soul, shared often with others (Matt. 18:19), simple and unpretentious in expression (like the "Lord's Prayer"), always submissive to God's overriding will and wisdom (Matt 6:10), and patient, because sometimes only time and repetition can purge the impulsiveness and shallowness of ill-considered requests (Luke 11:8-9). "The finest argument for a life of prayer is the praying Christ"; if he felt the need, so should we, and if he found it made a difference, so will we.

Equally clear, if we live under God's rule, is the need of *actual* obedience, not merely intellectual assent, to every principle, duty, counsel, and commandment of Jesus. "If any man's will is to do [God's] will, he shall know . . ." (John 7:17); much that puzzles us in the daily application of Christian ethics is not intellectual bewilderment but moral reluctance to obey. Ready obedience includes a humble submission to God's will when things "go wrong" — "things" being our plans, wishes, hopes, comfort, success, while the "going wrong" may in fact be the divine will for us. Such accepting faith is, very often, the deepest source of peace and of piety.

But our relation to God, Jesus says, must also involve love to our neighbor — "love," as always in such connections, meaning goodwill, the will to someone's good; and "neighbor" meaning (in Greek as in English) anyone near, close by, anyone within reach, anyone we may find on the road of life (as the good Samaritan did) in need of our influence or help or sympathy, however temporarily. That was Jesus' definition. It is deeply significant that this is a divine command, to which obedience is owed to God — not to society or even to the neighbor, who may in fact prove ungrateful, even resentful.

The plain and practical meaning of this unwearying goodwill is well expounded by Paul: "Owe no one anything, except to love one another; for he who loves his neighbor has fulfilled the law. The commandments, 'You shall not commit adultery, You shall not kill, You shall not steal, You shall not covet,' and any other commandment, are summed up in this sentence, 'You shall love your neighbor as yourself.' Love does no wrong to a neighbor; therefore love is the fulfilling of the law" (Rom. 13:8-10). Thus:

Such goodwill will never wrong another sexually, either the one already pledged to someone else, or that someone else. Indeed, the command to seek only another's good governs the whole Christian attitude to sex. Beginning from the principle that sex is sacred, since God created male and female and bisexual reproduction, and since the procreation of life is the very highest human capacity, the Christian will reverence at all times that natural purpose and avoid every exploitation of sexuality for monetary gain or for merely sensual pleasure, for the sake of his/her own purity and self-discipline and for others' sake, to avoid harming the health, self-discipline, purity, or social respect of any "partner." Even the desire for illicit sexual experience, nursed, fed, and persisted in for its own sake, is forbidden by Jesus (Matt. 5:28ff.) — evidently (from the context) because lust undermines the stern self-discipline he demands. Sexual experience within marriage is within God's purpose; its presuppositions are mutual love, tenderness, responsibility, and permanence (Matt. 19:3-9) — the sovereign demand for goodwill still applying. For those born with or acquiring later any irremovable obstacle to this divine purpose of procreation the Christian will feel only compassion and regret, never condemnation, while urging that the handicap be accepted, with God's grace, as other handicaps have to be, not indulged in ways harmful to others. As Paul implies, the one thing commanded in this field as in all others is unfaltering goodwill.

Such goodwill will never rob another of life, the means of life, the enjoyment of life, of health — the commandment is wide as life itself, excluding, as Jesus insists, injury, anger, resentment, revenge, retaliation, malice, and unforgivingness. Extremely difficult dilemmas arise when duty appears to demand military intervention to save others in danger or distress, or the ending of pregnancy to spare the too-young, raped, or too weak mother. Only those faced with such awful problems can decide where unfaltering goodwill will best be served, and for whom. Christians spared such agonizing questions can only sympathize.

Such goodwill will never rob another materially, seeking to deprive another of what is rightfully his/hers to enjoy, by theft, fraud, "sharp practice," deceit, or debt, for this is selfishness carried to its utmost. Love will not so much as envy or desire what is another's; "coveting" is mental stealing as lust is mental adultery. And the will to evil is evil, as truly as the will to good is virtuous. Paul has cited the entire "social table" of the commandments in Exodus 20, except for the prohibition of false witness; his "any other commandment" would certainly include that.

Such goodwill will never rob another of his/her good name or reputation, by slander libel, innuendo, or false accusation for whatever reason, nor misrepresent nor keep silent when loyal defense is called for. Unfaltering goodwill is a strict discipline for a too-free tongue.

But Paul's analysis of what violates love toward one's neighbor needs to be supplemented by Jesus' positive counsel and example, for love does not consist merely in "not doing any harm." Love's positive duties, as illustrated in several places, are indeed daunting, some frankly impossible for us, though not for Christ. In his sermon at Nazareth Jesus described his own ministry as bringing good news to the poor, release to captives, sight to the blind, liberty to the oppressed. In reporting his work to John the Baptist, Jesus mentioned also the cleansing of lepers, healing the deaf, raising the dead; and in the charge to his missioners he included healing the sick and exorcism. Luke's account adds preaching the kingdom, feeding the hungry, comforting the mourner, approaching the outcast insane, welcoming and blessing children, tending the injured by the road and arranging after-care even for chance strangers, seeking, saving and befriending the repentant sinful and despised, not condemning but counseling "sin no more," placating enemies, forgiving offenders.

Some of these ministries of love appear at once beyond both our ability and opportunity, though none are to be brushed aside as "impossible" without *something* we can do if we try. But admittedly it is something of a relief to hear Jesus base the final judgment not on such an exhaustive catalogue of duties, but upon the basics of feeding the hungry, refreshing the thirsty, welcoming the stranger, clothing the naked, visiting the sick and those in prison — and realizing that what is done in love for others is accepted as done for him (Matt. 25:31ff.).

At least we can attempt what is within our power; often we may find that such attempting leads to greater opportunities than we dreamed. The suggested measure of unfaltering love is simple: "as you love yourself," or in fuller form, "whatever you wish that men would do to you, do so to them; for this is the law and the prophets" (Matt. 7:12). And the motive? "As I have loved you."

Though the requirements of godliness, negative and positive, are not easy to fulfill, they must ever be seen in the light of God's presence and grace, of answered prayer and matchless hope, of daily renewed strength and often renewed joy. For godliness is not one-sided: as surely as we walk with God, he faithfully walks with us — however steep the road.

14

Jesus on Himself — and Us

M UCH OF WHAT Jesus taught about himself and what he means to those who follow him may be summarized by drawing together the remarkably varied titles he assumed or accepted from others. They include:

> *The Bridegroom,* whose gladdening presence makes fasting inappropriate for disciples, until he is taken away, and the bridegroom is "late" returning.
>
> *The Christ* (the Greek word for Messiah, the Anointed One; John 1:41) was the name Jesus accepted from Peter and used to identify himself to the woman of Samaria and on other occasions. In Jewish ears it was identified with nationalist hopes of the reestablishment of the Davidic dynasty of independent Jewish kings and the conception of an earthly kingdom of God that Jesus repudiated. Jesus therefore preferred other titles, and when Pilate challenged him as "Christ, a king," Jesus avoided direct reply — his kingship was not of this world.
>
> *The Coming One,* who will not leave disciples desolate but will come again, at some unforeseen hour, in glory, to reward his servants and sit in judgment — the Christ of the future.

The Counselor ("comforter" [John 14:16, 18, KJV] is Elizabethan English for one who fortifies). Jesus will not leave his people "comfortless"; God will send *another* counselor, advocate (RSV keeps the legal tone of ancient translators), or helper — quite literally one who comes alongside at times of need. The Spirit will be all that Jesus has been.

The Door of God's sheepfold by which his sheep obtain entrance, liberty ("to go in and out"), and satisfaction ("finding pasture").

The Good Shepherd, who seeks the lost sheep, gathers other sheep not of Israel, is smitten, leaving the sheep scattered (as was prophesied), and lays down his life for the sheep when the wolf comes, being no hireling. This (as we saw) echoes Ezekiel's promise that God himself shall shepherd Israel.

The Grain of Wheat which, unless it "falls into the earth and dies," remains fruitless; but if it does die, it bears much fruit.

Greater than Solomon, one whose appearance on the scene is as historic a moment as the reign of Israel's mightiest monarch — though Jesus is now despised.

The King (see Christ, "Messiah," above). Despite his reluctance to feed Jewish nationalism, Jesus fulfilled Zechariah's prophecy of the king upon a humble ass, accepted the title from Nathanael, implied his own royalty in discussing with Peter the payment of dues, and spoke of his coming throne.

The Life (John 14:6), as the bearer and giver of a new quality of life, "abundant," "eternal," the life that was "the light of men" showing what life could be like.

The Light of the World, so that disciples need not "walk in darkness," bringing light to those who sit in darkness, giving sight to the blind — the great enlightener of all willing to learn ("the world").

The Lord and teacher of the disciples, who must acknowledge no other (Matt. 23:8); Lord of the Sabbath, exemplifying right use of the day; the Lord who yet washes his disciples' feet; a title not to be used lightly (Matt. 7:21).

The Master of the disciples, linked with "Lord"; the word sometimes means teacher but also master of servants entrusted with
use of "talents" and care of his household.

The Messiah: see "Christ," "King" above.

"My Lord and my God," perhaps the most profound title Jesus accepted from anyone.

The Physician for those sick in soul, implied in Mark 2:17.

The Prophet not accepted in his own country who needs to go to
Jerusalem where prophets are killed. He cleanses the Temple,
quoting prophetic authority.

The Resurrection, one of his "I am" sayings; as giving eternal life,
even after death, and himself the first to rise from the dead.

The Servant of the Lord, fulfilling Isaiah's great prophecy of the
Servant who would bring good tidings to the afflicted, bind
up the brokenhearted, proclaim liberty and the year of the
Lord's favor; who would not strive or cry, nor break the
bruised reed nor quench the dimly burning wick, but establish
justice in the earth; who will grow up before God like a young
plant, but despised and rejected of men, who will be bruised
and put to grief, making himself an offering for sin, bearing
the sin of many, and being numbered with the transgressors;
"for the Son of man came not to be served but to serve, and to
give his life a ransom for many"; "I am among you as one who
serves."

The Son of David, which Jesus accepted when so appealed to for
help, but he resisted its popular connotations as nationalistic
and militaristic (Matt. 22:41-45).

The Son of God, accepted from Nathanael and after the stilling of
a storm; "Son of the Most High God" (Mark 5:7, probably in
a Greek-speaking area); very frequently implied in John's Gospel, as "Son of the Father."

The Son of man, Jesus' preferred title, occurring many times;
again from Ezekiel (who is so described more than eighty
times, as Jesus also is about eighty times), originally it proba-

bly meant simply "man," "human being" (Ps. 8:4, for example). But in Daniel's prophecy, following the reigns of the beasts there is to come a kingdom ruled by a son of man — a human realm (Daniel 7). Hence in later Jewish literature, "the Son of man" became a popular title for the (supernatural) Messiah coming in the clouds. Jesus may have used the title with Daniel's prophecy in mind but emphasizing his own humanity against "supernatural" hopes and his brotherhood with all men. As Son of man he claimed authority to forgive sins, was sociable (unlike the Baptist), would suffer, being "lifted up" in crucifixion, and would rise and come again in power.

The Sower casting the good seed of God's word into varying soils of men's hearts and into God's harvest fields (Matt. 13:37).

The Truth (John 14:6), as enshrining in himself — in all he said, all he did, all he was, all he suffered — the ultimate truth about God and human existence. For Jewish thinkers, "wisdom" was always ethical, not abstract philosophy, and truth always personal, not just right ideas. Jesus the truth expresses this perfectly.

The Vine of God, the Vinedresser, with disciples as branches to bear fruit for God, echoing Isaiah's parable of God's vineyard (commemorated on Judah's Temple gates and coins), which disappointed God, and Jesus' own parable on the same theme.

The Way (John 14:6) again reflects the Jewish emphasis on *ethical* thought about religion as "a path of life," "a daily walk," the broad and narrow ways open to choice, "the way of God . . . of salvation . . . of righteousness . . . the new and living way into the holiest." At first Christians were "people of the Way," and Christianity "the Way they call a sect," "the Way of peace." Jesus, in person, teaches, shows, and leads the way to God and heaven.

Thus Jesus frequently borrows ideas and titles already current in popular religious discourse and appropriates their deep emotional appeal while giving to each a deeper meaning, thus at once satisfying and transcending the people's expectation. The variety of such expressions serves to indicate Jesus' position, powers, and purposes from many viewpoints and succeeds in the end in proving him an "infinite" personality in the sense of being beyond all simple description, and certainly beyond precise definition. This, of course, is why he has been able to stimulate and satisfy the deepest faith and longings of succeeding generations worldwide.

These familiar titles, mainly from Matthew, Mark, and Luke, illustrate chiefly the relation of Jesus to ourselves; John's Gospel explores thoroughly the decades of reflection, against the background of Greek as well as Jewish thought, on the relation of Jesus to God. There is no reason to suppose that the later presentation of Christ's story falsifies its essential meaning if we do not overpress particular expressions, and more often than we may think, the earlier Gospels supply in simpler language parallels to John's thought.

The essence of John's testimony is that "No one has ever seen God; the only Son, who is in the bosom of the Father, he has made him known" (1:18). This is abundantly supported by Jesus' own words and the immense claims he made. The basis of Jesus' relation to God (he says) is simple: "The Father loves the Son . . . I love the Father" (four references). He came down from heaven, sent by the Father (twelve references), and will return to the Father. The Father bears witness to the Son, having sealed and consecrated him for his work (four references; Luke says, "and appointed him a kingdom"). God would have all men honor the Son.

So Jesus accepted the titles "Son of God" and "Son of the living God" (both from Matthew's Gospel). The relationship to God was as close as words can express: "I am in the Father and the Father in me"; "I am not alone, for the Father is with me"; "I live because of the Father"; "I and the Father are one"; "As Thou, Father, art in me, and I in Thee"; "Understand that the Father is in me, and I am in the Father"; "In that day you will know that I am in my Father, and you in me, and I in you" (seven references).

In consequence, Jesus can say, "No one comes to the Father but by me"; "All that the Father has is mine." Matthew preserves a similar claim: "No one knows the Son except the Father, and no one knows the Father except the Son and any one to whom the Son chooses to reveal him" (11:27).

Such claims sound exceedingly large and far-reaching until we place alongside them the complementary statements, equally repeated and equally emphasized in John's Gospel, in which Jesus disclaims personal greatness, ascribing all glory to the Father. When we consider the whole of Christ's teaching on his relation to God, it is evident that "in him God is glorified" (five references). "My Father is greater than I," Jesus insists, "greater than all." Only God the Father has the right to allot places of privilege in the kingdom, and only the Father knows the day and hour of the close of the age (Matt. 20:23, 24:3, 36). The absolute supremacy of the Father thus asserted involves the free acknowledgment of the Son's "subordination":

> *Jesus is under the Father's command* at all times, in all ways, doing "as the Father has commanded me," "keeping his commandments," "obeying his word" (four references).
>
> *Jesus has no will of his own.* "I seek not my own will"; "I have come not to do my own will"; "my food is to do the will of him who sent me"; "I always do what is pleasing to him."
>
> *Jesus has no initiative of his own.* "The Son can do nothing of his own accord" . . . "has not come of his own accord" (three references).
>
> *Jesus has no authority of his own.* "I do nothing on my own authority . . . I can do nothing"; "I have not spoken on my own authority"; "He whom God has sent utters the words of God" (five references).
>
> *Jesus has no message of his own.* "My teaching is not mine but his who sent me"; "I declare what I have heard from him"; "I speak thus as the Father taught me. . . the truth which I heard from God"; "the word which you hear is not mine but the Fa-

ther's"; "I have given them the words which Thou gavest me
. . . Thy word"; "The Father has himself given me commandment what to say . . . What I say therefore I say as the Father
has bidden me" (ten references).

Jesus exercises no judgment of his own. "The Father has given all
judgment to the Son . . . has given him authority to execute
judgment"; "As I hear I judge"; "I judge no one. Yet even if I
do judge, my judgment is true, for it is not I alone that judge,
but I and he who sent me" (four references).

Jesus does no works of his own. "My food is . . . to accomplish his
work"; "The Son can do . . only what he sees the Father doing, for whatever he does, that the Son does likewise"; "The
works which the Father has granted me to accomplish"; "Having accomplished the work which Thou gavest me to do" (five
references).

Jesus has no power of his own. "Thou hast *given* him power over all
flesh"; "The Father who dwells in me does his works . . . Believe the works that you may . . . understand that the Father is
in me, and I am in the Father."

Jesus seeks no glory of his own. "I do not seek my own glory"; "I do
not receive glory from men"; "He who seeks the glory of him
who sent him is true"; "Father, glorify Thy name" (five references).

Jesus has no life of his own. "I live because of the Father"; "As the
Father hath life in himself, so has he *granted* the Son also to
have life in himself"; "The Father . . . has given all things into
[the Son's] hand"; "They know that everything that Thou hast
given me is from thee" (four references).

All, thus, that Jesus has is God's free gift to Jesus. All these astonishing
statements are, according to John and his fellow-evangelists, from
Christ's own lips.

In the contrast between Christ's immense claims to close relation
with the Father and his surprising disclaimers of personal initiative

and glory we can measure the magnitude of his incarnation. Paul uses the expression "he emptied himself, taking the form of a servant" (Phil. 2:7), and the Gospels justify the bold statement. And justify, also, the declaration of John: "In the beginning was the Word, and the Word was with God, and the Word was God. . . . And the Word became flesh and dwelt among us, full of grace and truth."

A glance again over the varied titles of Jesus recalls the wonderful variety and completeness of the ministry Jesus offers us: the gifts of life to the full, enlightenment, liberty, security, sight, assurance, inner peace, the fellowship of the Spirit, answered prayer, renewal, refreshment, nourishment, guidance, forgiveness, a vocation worth pursuing, an ideal worth emulating, a friend beyond price, and immortality. Material wealth, safety, and advancement are *not* among Christ's promises, but sufficiency, spiritual security, survival, strength to endure, peace, and joy are ours if we have Christ. The realization of how utterly dependent he himself was upon the Father helps us conceive how nearly he came to our own life and circumstances, sharing fully in human experience and learning our needs, temptations, and frailty by sharing them.

On the other hand, his unique closeness to God explains the infinite resources with which he can meet our needs out of the wealth of divine strength and understanding thus available to him. In the most real sense Jesus is the way to the Father, the truth about the Father, and the expression of the life of the Father (John 14:6); he brings us God, as much of God as we are able to conceive or make our own. Jesus stands at the climax of long centuries of revelation, developing through history, law, prophecy, poetry, worship, and experience: when Jesus says "He that has seen me has seen the Father," the extended education of Israel in religion and ethics (and in principle of the world also) is completed. Though "no one has seen God at any time, the only begotten Son . . . has made God known." In this realm, as in all religious realms, Jesus is final: the rest of Christian history seeks to catch up with him and explore all that he offers, as his Spirit leads onward into "all the truth" (John 16:13).

The invitation to enter into all Christ offers is universal. As Jesus says, "This is the will of my Father, that *everyone* who sees the Son and believes in him should have eternal life . . . *Whoever* believes . . . *Whosoever* drinks of the water that I shall give him . . . *He who* hears my word and believes . . . *Everyone* then who hears these words and does them . . . *Everyone* who asks receives, *he who seeks* finds, *to him who knocks* it shall be opened." In the teaching of Jesus the unlimited opportunity is perfectly clear.

Of course there may be hindrances: habits to leave behind, memories and imagination to be cleansed, estrangement from God and things godly to be repaired. But Jesus repeatedly claims to have come not to call the righteous but sinners, to seek and to save the lost. The hindrance is always on our side, never on his. We may be unwilling to accept the consequences of loyalty to Christ, family divisions, social ostracism, persecution, the humiliation of penitent surrender to divine remaking. Jesus warns that we may prove ourselves "unworthy" after all if we love father or mother or others more than Christ or fail to take up our cross and follow in his steps. Jesus asks much. But remembering his crucifixion, we realize he deserves it all.

We do well to remember, too, that by our attitude to Jesus we reveal ourselves. Those "not of God," not "of the truth," do not come to Christ. Those who prefer darkness to light have something to hide. This is self-judgment, but also his judgment. There is no other who can save us from ourselves, and he is not to be trifled with any more than God is. Jesus speaks of our house of life falling in, of shut doors, of some told "I never knew you." But this outcome is no part of his purpose. His invitation stands, his promises are sure, his ability to save all who want to be saved is infinite. And once we place ourselves in his hands, he undertakes that none shall pluck us thence, nor from God's sure hold (John 10:27-30).

15

Jesus on the Future

O F ALL THE SUBJECTS on which Jesus spoke perhaps the most difficult to summarize clearly is the future unfolding of God's purpose. In part, this is because on this theme the meaning of figurative
language is most debatable: do eclipses, tumbling mountains, and the
moon turned to blood forecast literal convulsions of nature or are they
metaphors for upheavals in society or among world powers? Is "coming on the clouds of heaven" a prediction of an aerial landing or does it
mean simply "coming from God"? In part, too, the difficulty may be
due to the church's being herself unclear, by the time the Gospels were
written, just what Jesus meant. Certainly Paul at one time thought the
return of Jesus was so imminent that there was no time for the slave to
seek freedom or for the single to marry (1 Cor. 7:17-29). Yet Matthew,
in the eighth decade, is still recalling sayings that end with "the end is
not yet."

On this theme, the old maxim still applies: "Prophecy is best understood when it has been fulfilled."

About a few coming events, Jesus' teaching was unmistakable.
Among these, one was his own death. Mark records, as early in his
Gospel as 3:6, a decision to kill Jesus. Each Gospel writer arranges his
material to suit his purposes; Mark has arranged together five stories

illustrating why Jesus was opposed. It seems clear, however, that Jesus spoke early of his being taken, as the bridegroom, from his guests, and their fasting in consequence; later, of his having to fall, like seed, into the ground to bear fruit; of being "lifted up" to draw all men unto him, meaning upon a cross; and of going away, going to the Father. Toward the end, Jesus speaks of being anointed for burial, and of the shepherd being smitten, the sheep scattered. All four Gospels record Jesus' words about betrayal; some reference to return or resurrection often accompanies the prophecy.

Such forecasts imply that Jesus' death would be no mistake, defeat, failure, or unforeseen tragedy, but part of the divine purpose of his coming. Was it not necessary, he asks, "that the Christ should suffer?" . . . "to give his life a ransom for many" . . . "that repentance and forgiveness of sin might be preached in his name to all nations." The transformation of the cross in the eyes of the disciples, from the bewildering tragedy discussed by two walking to Emmaus into the central theme of the "good news" preached everywhere by the church, is a strong strand in the evidence that Christ rose again.

Clear, too, is Jesus' vision of the fate of Israel. Not only is the vineyard of God to pass to other tenants, and the literal kingdom that Jews expected a Davidic Messiah to establish replaced by a spiritual kingdom of hearts obedient to divine rule, but the land and nation of Israel will be destroyed. "The blood of all the prophets . . . shall be required of this generation," Jesus said. "O Jerusalem, Jerusalem, killing the prophets . . . How often would I have gathered your children together as a hen gathers her brood under her wings, and you would not! Behold, your house [the Temple] is forsaken."

Responding to the disciples' admiration of the Temple, Jesus said, "There will not be left here one stone upon another. . . ." Later he urged, "Daughters of Jerusalem, do not weep for me, but weep for yourselves and for your children. For behold, the days are coming when they will say, 'Blessed are the barren.'" He himself had earlier wept over Jerusalem, saying, "Would that even today you knew the things that make for peace!" as he vividly foresaw the horrors of a siege, the sign of desolation prophesied by Daniel, and other accompanying features of the end. His counsel, to seek safety in the surrounding hills, shows that it is of the fate of Judea that he is thinking. By the time Matthew and Luke recorded these prophecies, the Romans had burned the Temple, destroyed the city, and banished Jews from the Holy Land. But at the time Jesus had spoken them, such prophecies were in Jewish ears sheer blasphemy.

Jesus is equally sure of the ultimate establishment of God's kingdom. Already during his ministry it is "at hand," publicans and harlots enter it, the childlike belong to it, and when Pharisees demand when the kingdom will appear they are told it is in their midst, unrecognized. In spite of this, Jesus could speak of a coming manifestation of God's rule: "There are some standing here who will not taste of death before they see the kingdom of God come *with power* (Mark 9:1; Matthew has "see the Son of man coming in his kingdom"). Jesus was confident that God's rule was both come, and coming — already come in believing and submissive hearts, still coming in ever widening fulfillment. It is "not of this world" in origin (as though men must build it; John 18:36), nor is it for Jesus himself to appoint places of privilege in it; that is the prerogative of the kingly Father. But he promised solemnly at the last supper with his men to drink wine with them again in the Father's kingdom.

A fourth clear theme concerning the future is Jesus' own coming again, though this does become somewhat confused with "the end of the world" (RSV "the close of the age"). According to Matthew's great "discourse" (collected sayings) about the future (Matt. 24-25), the disciples asked a threefold question: "When will this [the destruction of the Temple] be, and what will be the signs of both your coming and of the close of the age?" The "discourse" touches at places on each point. Of the end we know little except that there will be a harvest, and a judgment. The return of Jesus will become a matter of endless speculation and false rumors, but that he will come again is certain. "I will not leave you desolate; I will come to you . . . I will see you again . . . Hereafter you will see the Son of man seated at the right hand of power and coming on the clouds of heaven"; similar imagery is repeated several times. It helps little to say that the clouds, angels, and trumpets are traditional in Jewish apocalyptic writing; the problem remains how to interpret such language, for Jesus was no apocalyptist.

Along with the certainty of Christ's return is our ignorance of the time. Mark records the surprising admission, "But of that day or that hour no one knows, not even the angels in heaven, *nor the Son,* but only the Father" . . . "you do not know when the time will come" (13:32ff.). The days of Noah are recalled, when people went about their daily lives unheeding; "they did not know until the flood came." So it will be with the coming of Christ. The unforeseen entry of a thief, the suddenness of lightning, the surprise of a snare, the unexpectedness of the lava storm on Sodom — all are compared to the unheralded arrival of Jesus.

On the other hand, despite our ignorance of the time, certain warnings are given. Matthew insists, for his eighth-decade readers, "the end is not yet," listing fourteen things that must happen: wars, rumors of wars, famines, earthquakes, love growing cold; "all this is but the beginning of the sufferings . . . then the end will come" (Matt. 24:4-14). These events, like the tendering of the stems and leaves of the fig tree heralding summer, are signs that "he is near." Others, who supposed that the kingdom would immediately appear as Jesus neared Jerusalem, were warned of the need to trade faithfully with the resources entrusted to them, while the kingdom waited.

The spiritual value, perhaps the purpose, of this ambiguous uncertainty lies in the repeated call to be prepared. Christ's servants must be "girded, with lit lamps," "like men waiting for their master to come home from the marriage feast, that they may open to him at once . . . Blessed are those servants whom the master finds awake." The parable of the wise and foolish bridesmaids teaches the same lesson of readiness for the unknown hour; that of the talents suggests that the best preparation is to serve in the master's absence with diligence and courage. Through all this prophecy the constant refrain is, "Watch": "What I say to you I say to all, 'Watch.'" "Watch at all times, praying that you may have strength to escape all these things that will take place, and to stand before the Son of man."

Some have found it possible to argue that, figurative language notwithstanding, Jesus *did* return, in the Spirit, to his church at Pentecost; his saying that "some standing here" would see the kingdom come in power was thus fulfilled. Others find this quite unconvincing, especially as Matthew and Luke do not suggest anything of the kind. These still look for a literal and personal return of Christ to earth; of course any such return could not but be personal. The difficulty is to understand his physical presence after so long. Certainly we must not emphasize Christ's *coming* in any way that obscures his *presence* with us already. For the rest, we must wait and see.

In short: for the disciple the hope of Christ's coming and kingdom is invincible; some ignorance is humbling but unavoidable; *readiness is all.*

On the future of the individual Jesus has rather less to say, though what is said is momentous. An afterlife is described in traditional terms: an extreme punishment where deserved, "the hell of fire"; "in Hades, in torment"; seeing "the comfort" of "Abraham's bosom a great way off"; "a day of judgment"; but for others, "paradise" (a garden); "my Father's kingdom"; "heaven"; "that where I am there you may be also," the place of reunion. Jesus told certain Sadducees that the afterlife knows neither marriage nor giving in marriage, Luke adding "for they cannot die any more." There is a hint of "timelessness" in the warning about some seeing Abraham, Isaac, and Jacob and all the prophets in the kingdom of God, and ourselves shut out. This is present too in the assertion that Moses showed that the dead are raised when he wrote of God as God of Abraham, Isaac, and Jacob, the God of the living, not of the dead, for all live unto him. We hear also of "eternal habitations" (Luke 16:9).

The words of Jesus to the thief dying beside him have a special value for Christian hearts, though we wish we understood more exactly what they mean: "today," "with me," "in paradise" — each phrase is full of promise. Does Jesus imply no intermediate waiting for

a day of resurrection? Matthew's curious story of the tombs broken
open by the earthquake at Jesus' crucifixion, when "many bodies of the
saints who had fallen asleep were raised, and coming out of the tombs
after his resurrection they went into the holy city and appeared to
many," raises more questions than it answers.

The emphasis on this theme in the earlier Gospels falls instead
upon the resurrection of Jesus, prepared for in some degree by his own
recalling of others to life. "He is not here . . . he has risen" is history's
supreme announcement of man's immortality. Luke, a physician, records faithfully the signs of restored life offered to doubtful Thomas.
Matthew, Mark, and Luke make this stupendous fact the climax of
their story — what could they add? Luke especially dwells upon the
scene in the garden, with the faithful women who expected to anoint
Christ's body; upon the two walking to Emmaus with the risen Lord
out of bewildered despair into shining certainty; upon Jesus' appearance with enlightenment to his grieving men at Jerusalem, and then at
Bethany. This is the sure foundation of the apostolic confidence that
Jesus had "abolished death," that "death no more held dominion" but
was "swallowed up in victory"; that in fact death is now "ours," the last
enemy to be destroyed (2 Tim. 1:10, Rom. 6:9, 1 Cor. 15:54, 3:22,
15:26).

Last came John's Gospel, almost a meditation upon everlasting
life, which he refers to in various ways some thirty-three times. Some
of the utterances John has preserved for us are breathtaking. "Truly,
truly, I say to you, if any one keeps my word he will never see death";
"he who hears my word and believes him who sent me has eternal life";
my sheep hear my voice, and I know them . . . and I give them eternal
life, and they shall never perish"; "this is the will of him who sent me,
that every one who sees the Son and believes in him should have eternal life, and I will raise him up at the last day"; "In my Father's house
are many rooms . . . I go to prepare a place for you . . . that where I am
you may be also"; "I am the resurrection and the life; he who believes
in me, though he die, yet shall he live, and whoever lives and believes
in me shall never die."

John, too, has that unforgettable scene in the garden of the tomb, when Jesus twice asks the significant question, "Woman, why are you weeping?"; and the scene by the lake where the risen Jesus asks Peter, "Do you love me?" — the two final questions posed by the whole marvelous gospel of everlasting life. It is John, too, who has preserved the ultimate, unanswerable argument of Jesus, "Because I live, you will live also."

These are but a selection of the many and varied assurances in the Gospels that the future for the Christian believer is bright with hope and infinite promise. Of course there remain questions and difficulties: the truth is too big to believe, yet too big to be untrue, too vital to surrender. Some odd ambiguities demand care: the promise that believers "shall never die" cannot be taken literally in view of the generations that have passed, and had already passed even when John wrote. We mentally interpret the words to mean "shall never really, finally die" — since they will rise again. We know, too, that "eternal life," like "life . . . abundantly" (John 10:10), describes the quality of life that Jesus bestows now, as well as its duration. It is life worth lasting forever.

This again, for modern minds, demands an effort of faith. It is well to realize that the difficulty we feel is a problem not of reason but of imagination — the impossibility of picturing to ourselves a realm where all who have lived live again. Reason is quite as reluctant to accept that all the long story of the universe — orderly, developing, producing life, beauty, rationality, consciousness, science, heroism, values, itself amazingly complex yet amenable to scientific explanation — must end in irrational chaos and nothingness, without meaning, purpose, or achievement. That is as hard for sense and morality to accept as the aim, the explanation, and the meaning of it all as it is to accept the invincible hope that the end will be otherwise.

On the other hand, the limits of human imagination are *not* the limits of human experience. Everyone who reads these words *has already* spent most of a year in total darkness, gradually becoming aware of warmth, movement, rhythm, but utterly, absolutely unable to imagine a world of sun and wind, stars, mountains and seas, people, buses, planes, and populated cities, colors, scents, voices, music, tastes. Yet on a sudden day he or she *has already passed* that barrier of the unimaginable, arriving in just such a world. If it can be done once, why, *rationally* why, not again?

Through all our doubts, our striving to grasp and simplify and imagine, there still shines the wondering hope that gives meaning and value to our present lives — and for Christians, the glorious certainty that Thomas in his questioning doubt discovered to his heart's great comfort. When we accept Jesus' invitation to draw near and then put out our hand and, touching, know that before us is life in living contact with a risen Savior, we too can only gasp, "My Lord and my God!"